PRAISE FOR *GREAT WORK*

David Sturt's *Great Work* is brilliantly conceived, expertly executed, and powerfully motivating. Just two chapters into the book I found myself scribbling down my own ideas to make a difference people love. *Great Work* is a great work.

Richard Paul Evans
#1 *New York Times*, *Wall Street Journal*, and
USA Today bestselling author

Great Work funnels a vast amount of research into sensible, readable vignettes that resonate with the day-to-day challenges faced by operating managers. Using stories, Sturt pulls the reader into situations that he will certainly recognize. The result evolves into a leadership framework that is practical, memorable, and useful. If you aspire to lead a team to greatness, *Great Work* should be your handbook.

Gary Crittenden
CEO and Managing Partner, HGGC
Former CFO of Citigroup, American Express, Monsanto, Sears

Great work is not driven by what you are, but rather by what you *do*. You don't need an outsized personality, an enormously high IQ, or a killer presentation style. You don't need to become someone you are not. Apply the principles found in this book and discover remarkable dreams are truly within your reach.

Whitney Johnson
author of *Dare, Dream, Do: Remarkable Things
Happen When You Dare to Dream*
Harvard Business Review contributor

Great Work captures the heart and mind of the reader through the deeds of ordinary people doing extraordinary work. A quick read that provides sound research on the paradigms and patterns of thinking and behaving that result in *Great Work*. If you are looking for breakthrough innovation and creativity from your people or they are looking at you for this kind of leadership, then you'll want to read this book. So simple, but yet so powerful!!!

Tom Carroll
EVP Chief Human Resources Officer
RR Donnelley

This business book invoked a wide range of feelings . . . from inspired and ignited to tear-infused and thought-provoking. It fed my soul, spirit, and business acumen all at the same time.

David Sturt celebrates and calls each of us as people and leaders to look for the difference we can create and deliver. No matter the role or title of our work, these stories connect us to inspire, transform, and lead.

Humans are our world's greatest resource and innovation is humanity's best tool; thanks to David Sturt for shining the light on common people making an uncommon difference.

Great inspiration; great business; great impact; *GREAT WORK*!

Dana Ullom-Vucelich
Chief Human Resources Officer, OPRS

We all know difference makers who, in small ways, make a profound impact on how we work and live. Thanks to David Sturt and O.C. Tanner Institute for helping us recognize and celebrate them.

Tom Post
Managing Editor
Forbes Media

As an individual who has experienced and surpassed many obstacles in order to achieve my own dreams of accomplishing *Great Work*, I am highly compelled by this new book and by the new research that it represents. I recommend it to everyone, from every background, who is inspired by the idea of having remarkable dreams to achieve.

Barbara Corcoran
The Corcoran Group—real estate mogul, business expert,
and a "Shark" on ABC's hit series *Shark Tank*

Great Work is a great work. It captures how people and organizations can help their employees have both passion and productivity at work. The five tools (ask, see, talk, improve the mix, and deliver) are well grounded in research and practice. The marvelous stories bring the ideas to life and offer specific tools any employee or leader can use. The ideas in the book educate, inspire, and capture the essence of a new way to produce great work.

Dave Ulrich
Professor, Ross School of Business, University of Michigan
Partner, The RBL Group

I was so inspired by this book. I felt this surge of excitement, energy, perseverance, and passion from so many case studies that I feel I could take my work beyond great. I always have the greatest faith in humanity, that we are capable of anything, but in order to do that it takes the passion, risk, foresight, rigor, and perseverance to think outside the box . . . to think beyond status quo, seeing problems as opportunities, to leap into contributing great work to the world. This book is a fabulous inspiration and methodology for exactly that. There is nothing greater than great work.

Karim Rashid
Internationally recognized designer

Tremendous! This masterful piece of research in story form has us asking the right questions to orient ourselves before getting started. It has us talking to our outer circle in a world that sorely needs broader collaboration and greater trust. It has us seeing new things and looking at our work with new eyes. *Great Work* has me believing anyone can deliver a difference—and I predict that "making a difference people love" will embed itself in our lexicon for decades to come.

Stephen M. R. Covey
author of the *New York Times* and
1 *Wall Street Journal* bestseller
The Speed of Trust

GREAT
WORK

GREAT WORK

HOW TO MAKE A
DIFFERENCE PEOPLE LOVE

DAVID STURT

O.C. TANNER INSTITUTE

Mc
Graw
Hill
Education

New York   Chicago   San Francisco   Athens   London   Madrid
Mexico City   Milan   New Delhi   Singapore   Sydney   Toronto

1 2 3 4 5 6 7 8 9 0   DOC/DOC   1 9 8 7 6 5 4 3

ISBN: 978-0-07-181835-3
MHID: 0-07-181835-9

e-ISBN: 978-0-07-181840-7
e-ISBN: 0-07-181840-5

McGraw-Hill Education books are available at special quantity discounts to use as premiums and sales promotions or for use in corporate training programs. To contact a representative, please visit the Contact Us pages at www.mhprofessional.com.

This book is printed on acid-free paper.

TO THE THOUSANDS OF PEOPLE

WHOSE GREAT WORK INSPIRED US

TO WRITE THIS BOOK

CONTENTS

THE INCREDIBLE DISAPPEARING SCHOOL

"To lose your school is to lose your identity as a town," says Newcomb Town Supervisor George Canon.

Newcomb, New York, is a 255-mile road trip from Manhattan, but it might as well be a million miles away. The sportsman's paradise sits inside Adirondack Park, 59 miles from Burlington, Vermont, and includes the Lake Harris campground and about 481 residents.

If you look at satellite images of Newcomb on Google Maps, all you can see are lakes, trees, and the Newcomb School playground. It's as if the surrounding forest is trying to swallow the school and return to the days of the Iroquois and Algonquin tribes.

On June 13, 2006, Clark "Skip" Hults got the call he had been waiting for. A big fan of the North Country since visits in his youth, he was pleased to have been hired as the new superintendent of Newcomb Central School.

"The board members had seen my success in reaching out to less advantaged students in southern New York," Skip says. "So they hired me for fresh thinking—mostly in the area of administrative programs and academic excellence, stuff like that."

So Skip moved to the North Country and settled in to the usual superintendent duties: everything from drawing curriculum maps to meeting with students who needed discipline to paying the bills. Skip was happy to do these things, but he had also hoped to affect the school and the community he loved in a more meaningful way.

When Skip arrived in 2006, Newcomb Central School's population, like the town's, had been shrinking steadily ever since local logging and mining industries began to leave Newcomb in the late 1970s. Only 57 students were enrolled in all 13 grades (preschool through twelfth grade). After serving 350 students at its peak, the school was nearing the end of a 40-year decline that would probably result in the kids being bused elsewhere. The week Skip started, two more kids moved away, lowering the total student count to 55.

But there wasn't much talk about tackling that problem.

What was the point?

Skip explains, "When I first came, the school's shrinking enrollment was so ingrained that it had become invisible. Big problems are like that. Your eyes are sometimes closed to them because if you acknowledge them, you have to deal with them. And that might seem impossible. Most rural schools simply give up. It's the norm in many professions to accept the most broken things of all as unfixable and work on everything else instead."

Although no one assigned Skip the task of increasing enrollment, he surveyed the situation and thought, "We need to grow." But how? He couldn't exactly bring back the logging and mining industries of the past. Nor could he easily nab students from surrounding towns. How could he attract more students to a tiny, remote public school? What would help the school become a magnet for new students? And from where?

What could his school possibly offer that would be different from other schools in the area?

Meanwhile, a different problem was nagging at Skip's subconscious: Newcomb's lack of diversity. Having moved from an urban school with more than 80 percent minority students, his daughter once called her rural school "vanilla" because of its single-race population. "Everyone is just like me," she said. And she didn't mean it in a good way. Skip's family understood that students leave small towns like Newcomb (where 95 percent of the residents are Caucasian) to enter a business world filled with multiple languages, multiple cultures, multiple religions, and multiple points of view. How prepared would the town's kids be to collaborate, compete, and market themselves in an increasingly global world?

Skip accepted Newcomb Central School's declining enrollment as his own personal problem to solve. But even after he had been looking for solutions for some time, answers were hard to come by. Then one day, as he was talking about education on the phone with his brother in Australia, inspiration struck. Skip's brother, a recruiter of international students for private schools, simply mentioned in passing that educating international students is the third largest industry in Australia.

Wait. Say that again. Really?

Skip suddenly saw the planets align between his small town public school's need for diversity and its need for more students. That unexpected connection helped him imagine a simple solution:

Rural school + international students = growth.

Skip was hit with a sudden wave of feasibility. He could imagine how adding international students might change Newcomb's future.

Growth-wise, even just three or four new students a year would reverse the negative flow from the year before. And what might students from other countries add to the small town in terms of diversity, cultural perspective, language exposure, academic mentoring, and social life? Considering that potential change, Skip could see that there would be no new costs. The school already had the teachers, the desks, the textbooks, and the staff. All it would need were consumables like food and housing. The benefits were almost certain to outweigh the costs. Skip still had more questions than answers, but he believed his idea was inherently doable. So he began to share his idea with those whose support he would need to make it happen. Town leaders and school faculty got on board. Residents came forward as host families. And happen it did.

OUTCOMES AND RIPPLES

Over the last five years, Newcomb Central School has welcomed 61 students from 25 different nations, including Germany, France, China, Sweden, Brazil, Bangladesh, Zimbabwe, Serbia, Israel, Switzerland, South Korea, Iraq, Suriname, Lebanon, Australia, Japan, Finland, Thailand, Vietnam, Russia, Armenia, Spain, and Uruguay.

In casual conversation, Skip seems more enamored with the upswing in diversity than with the growth. "Imagine, in our small rural town, a social studies discussion where a Christian Palestinian living in Israel shares what it's like to be hated equally by Jews and Palestinians because of his religious beliefs.

"We've had a young girl from Baghdad explain how she saw people killed, and how she slept with her clothes on so that she could flee her home in the middle of the night if necessary.

"We've had Muslims and Buddhists in our school—something that just didn't use to happen in the North Country.

"Then you add the overall brightness of these kids and their impact on our math and science discussions. It's enriching our classrooms beyond measure."

The improvement hasn't gone unnoticed by surrounding communities. The by-product that Skip wasn't expecting from the program was 84 percent growth in just five years. "The reputation and quality of the international program have caused kids to commute in from out of town," Skip says. "A few new families have moved in. Some out-of-town students are staying with grandparents or aunts and uncles to study in Newcomb. One man, who was a town supervisor elsewhere, gave up reelection in his town and moved his family to Newcomb so his kids could switch schools. In 2012, Newcomb Central School celebrated hitting the 100-student mark for the first time since the 1980s with a potluck dinner in the cafeteria.

Skip now consults with school boards nationwide and at least a dozen rural school superintendents who at first scoffed at his idea. Educators from China and Russia have traveled to Newcomb to visit and learn from a successful American educational system. "Parents everywhere want their kids ready for life in the real world," Skip says, "and international programs are making that happen. Our school, which never used to make it into the newspaper in Glens Falls, has now been covered by the BBC, Reuters, and the Associated Press."

The foreign students who made all of this possible have benefited as well. "Kids don't just go to school here," Skip says. "They socialize and date one another, play sports, act in the school play, and become a part of our town family. They hike and ski and snowmobile. They make friends." One student came from Bangladesh, from a city of 30 million. At first he couldn't sleep. He hated it. There was no traffic, no noise, no city, no shopping. But he adjusted. And thrived. "When it came time to leave," Skip says, "no student cried more than he did."

GREAT WORK IS MAKING A DIFFERENCE PEOPLE LOVE

Skip's addition of international students to his rural school was brilliant. It works. It's proven. It has affected hundreds of students and their families academically, socially, and economically beyond what anyone could have imagined.

To the students, the difference is cool new friends to hang out with, exposure to other cultures, a better overall education, and critical mass for school activities (dances, sports, school plays, and so on).

To the parents, the difference is not having to have their kids bused elsewhere, the opportunity to become a host family, and all of those differences that the international students have made for their kids.

To the teachers, the difference is diversity, greater resources, greater class participation, and job security.

To the town leaders, the difference is a growing, vibrant community, stable property values, and all the advantages that come with having, rather than losing, a town school.

To Skip's peers at other small town schools, the difference is hope—that something *can* be done about declining town populations, lack of diversity, and school closures.

Finally, by making a difference for all those people, Skip is making a difference for himself as well. He loves his work. He takes pride in it. He's gained new friends on a global scale, has a sense of fulfillment, and has had a positive influence on education far beyond his hometown.

Great Work is a book about creating differences people love. Not only big, life-changing differences like Skip's, but small and medium-sized ones as well. We'll take a look at work that's making a difference in education, technology, healthcare, manufacturing, engineering, and dozens of other industries. Join us to explore how people find creative ways to write another page in the book of human progress. We'll learn how difference makers think and what they do. But as we go forward, there is something important you should know: the most significant examples of great work, the most poignant, the most inspiring, the ones we know would take your breath away, we can't tell you about. They haven't happened yet. They're yours.

Meet Skip Hults and hear the story of Newcomb Central School in a video by visiting greatwork.com or attending one of our workshops.

WHERE THIS BOOK
COMES FROM

A group of O.C. Tanner Institute members and partners, incuding researchers, business leaders, writers, designers, and academics, were working with the world's largest employee recognition company when we began asking some interesting questions: What does great work look like? Where does it come from? Why are some people so good at accomplishing it? While thinking about these questions, we realized that we were sitting on one of the world's largest databases of award-winning work. This got us thinking: Might these records tell us something about people who make a difference? Do award-winning employees do anything unusual that could help us do great work? Could knowing their secrets help other people do award-winning work? What might we learn from focusing on great work and then looking back at what people did to accomplish it?

With these questions in mind, we were now beyond curious to find out what people were doing whenever great work was achieved. We simply had to know. There was no turning back.

We enlisted two academics with PhDs from Harvard and Cambridge to help us design a research methodology for the largest-ever study of award-winning work. We interviewed experts, reviewed third-party research and literature, and conducted a survey of executives to develop several hypothesis. Then we began the study with more than five million written accounts of great work. These accounts came in the form of electronic nominations, written by supervisors or colleagues to rec-ommend someone for a corporate award as described in Appendix B. To arrive at exclusively award-winning work, we isolated 1.7 million nomi-nation records where an actual award was received. Then came the real task: to read and analyze a random sample of 10,000 of these accounts of award-winning work and code the contents into specific categories of attitudes, skills, and behaviors.

As we started to study the coded data, a small number of activities that influence great work began to emerge. We saw patterns that gave us insights into where great work comes from. We ran correlation and regression models. What interested us most was that the factors that appeared to have an impact on great work were actionable skills that anyone could perform.

We also worked with Forbes Insights to do an extensive analysis of more than 1,000 employees, supervisors, and work beneficiaries to val-idate our findings and get a more holistic view of people's work. Forbes asked these people to think about what behaviors were present during a specific project delivered in the last three months. Because the projects varied from poor work to great work, we were able not only to draw a second perspective on which behaviors influence great work, but also to see which behaviors influenced good work and poor work. As we tested these principles against interviews with more academics and third-party research, we continued to distill the foundational principles of great work, trimming those that were unimportant and collapsing those with similar traits into one. We found ourselves saying things like, "Oh, wow; this is what's going on," "Look at this; it's showing up everywhere," and "Aha, so this is what they really did."

By far, one of the most insightful aspects of our research was more than 200 one-on-one interviews. We spoke with more than 200 difference makers: people from diverse backgrounds, from entry-level workers to senior executives, whose only common denominator was that they had done some undeniably great work. We conducted another survey of 300 CEOs to get their perspective on great work. Along the way, we read and studied hundreds of accounts of people who had made a difference throughout history. As we met with difference makers—seeing their impact and being delighted by their improvements—they inspired and enlightened us. They blew us away. After all our research, it was difference makers themselves who schooled us on where great work comes from, adding profound insights, useful details, and friendly assists along the way.

In the end, we distilled our findings into two distinct categories: how difference makers think and what they do.

GREAT WORK

HOW DIFFERENCE MAKERS THINK

CHAPTER 1

REFRAME YOUR ROLE

THE ROLE OF A DIFFERENCE MAKER

IS AVAILABLE TO EVERYONE.

Anyone can be a difference maker. That said, there is something surprising about the way we think about ourselves when we're in a difference-making mode. Our mindset shifts from seeing ourselves as workers with an assignment to crank out to seeing ourselves as people with a difference to make. This shift is easy to identify in a person we interviewed named Ed.

In the spring of 1986, Ed landed his first grown-up job: selling airtime for a local AM radio station. His new position was anything but glamorous. Ed's colleagues at the station, where he had begun a year earlier emptying trash cans, congratulated him on his "step down" from janitor to sales. By all appearances, Ed was just another eager upstart: young and inexperienced, with no client list to speak of except the phone book his boss had handed him when he was hired, along with the words, "Go get 'em."

In our interview with Ed, he shared with us how he did what every John, Dick, Harry, Jane, Jill, and Mary does when he or she first gets a break in sales. He pounded the pavement (or drove it, rather—in a red

1962 VW Beetle with no air conditioning and the heater stuck on high). It was the dead of summer, and the windows were stuck shut. Ed told us, "Day after day, I sweltered in my car and hawked the benefits of radio to prospective clients in treeless strip malls and asphalt-and-stucco industrial complexes. I had a recurring nightmare that I wouldn't meet my quota." Ed sold plumbers and dry cleaners on the virtues of radio advertising rather than using newspaper, billboards, or TV. Months went by, and Ed had no contracts of any value (just a small carpet store or two), while all the senior reps at the station kicked back on the gravy train of well-established client relationships.

Great work didn't seem possible here—not when the old guard had all the big clients and the new guard had no clue. But then Ed attended a sales seminar. And while most of the information there was merely sales shtick, there was a simple story, told by one of the presenters, that transformed the way Ed thought about his seemingly dead-end job.

As the story goes, a radio sales rep just like Ed walked into a neighborhood video store to sell some advertising. But the owner of the video store stopped him cold and said, "I'm sorry, but you'll have to come back in six months. I'm moving to a new location, and the move will take every penny I can spare. I can't waste money on radio ads telling customers to come to this store when it won't even be here in just a few weeks."

So the sales rep went back to his radio station dejected.

But something kept nagging at him: a hunch. A voice inside that said, "I can figure this out. There has to be some way radio advertising can help that store owner right now." That got him thinking differently. Or rather, thinking about how to make a difference. New ideas began to percolate, and one, in particular, grabbed hold, felt right, and got him excited. So he returned to the video store owner and said: "Here's an idea: give me your entire moving budget to spend on radio ads. We'll run a promotion offering free videos to customers if they pick the movies up at your current store and return them to your new one." The owner went nuts for the idea. The rep landed the sale, and the two of them went to work.

Did the idea make a difference?

Yes, yes, yes, and yes. The overall cost of the radio campaign was a mere pittance compared to the upside. The store's customers were thrilled by the free videos, and they actually got a kick out of helping with the move. The store owner was ecstatic because 90 percent of his inventory was moved by his customers instead of a moving truck—not to mention that he no longer needed to advertise his new location because his most loyal customers had already made a visit. The radio rep landed more than just a sale; he landed a customer who saw him as a trusted marketing advisor. Of course, the station manager was equally elated to have a new longstanding client. Win. Win. Win. And win.

DIFFERENCE MAKING IS CONTAGIOUS

After hearing this success story, Ed returned to his radio station with a new energy about how he could find ways to make a difference. He didn't know exactly what that might mean. But the video-moving story had taught him something significant. "I'd been thinking about my job in such a limited, expected way," says Ed. "I'd agreed to build a client base by cold-calling businesses around town, a technique the senior reps had a monopoly on. I would always be a small fish in their pond because they

owned the pond. The question was: Could I find a new way to delight customers? Could I create my own pond?"

So 24-year-old Ed, rookie radio rep, started to look for difference-
making opportunities. He wanted to do more than just make a sale. He
wanted to become a trusted advisor who helped businesses thrive. Ed
quickly came up with a handful of good ideas for ways he could make
a difference. But the most inspired, the most unexpected, and on paper
the most far-fetched was his idea of going after big-budget clients who
up to that point had refused to advertise on radio ever.

He started looking at different industries and making new connections, and what he learned was that there were gigantic ad budgets in
food brokerage, that brokers had lucrative co-op deals with their manufacturers, and that the reason these brokers didn't buy radio ads was that
they didn't think radio could give them the same measurable results as
coupon-driven print ads. Hmm.

What did Ed do with all that information?

He joined the food brokers association. He made friends with brokers
all over the city. He talked to prospective clients, not to make a sale initially, but to understand their business, their goals, and their advertising
needs. He brainstormed ways in which radio ads could yield measurable results. He built relationships with local ad agencies. He stopped
seeing other media, such as coupons and print ads, as competition to be
eliminated and began to suggest that the brokers use coupons in *combination* with radio to get better results. He even suggested small advertising buys on other radio stations to reach customers that his station
could not. In time, the days of signing little deals with the likes of Bob's
Carpet Barn gave way to lucrative deals with some of the largest adver-

tisers in the city. Ed took food brokers ideas they loved. They agreed to give radio a try. It worked. And many businesses that had long snubbed radio advertising gradually became Ed's loyal clientele, his own pond. The food brokers' sales increased. Their customer awareness improved. Their companies thrived. And their appreciation for Ed grew with every radio ad that hit the airwaves.

Three years later, Ed left the station as the number one sales rep. The veteran sales reps with their longstanding client lists had been beaten by a 27-year-old kid with a phone book who chose to make a difference.

JOB CRAFTING

University of Michigan professor Jane Dutton has done extensive research into what makes people like Ed rethink their roles so capably.

Back in 2001, Jane and a colleague, Amy Wrzesniewski from Yale, began to study how people in unglamorous jobs were coping with what they called "devalued work." When they tried to think of supposedly unrewarding jobs to study, they chose hospital janitors. But what they learned from their studies took them completely by surprise and changed the trajectory of their research for the coming decade.

As Jane and Amy interviewed the cleaning staff of a major hospital in the Midwest, they discovered that a certain subset of housekeepers didn't see themselves as part of the janitorial staff at all. They saw themselves as part of the professional staff, as part of the healing team. And that changed everything. These people would get to know the patients and their families and would offer support in small but important ways:

a box of Kleenex here, a glass of water there, or a word of encouragement. One housekeeper reported rearranging pictures on the walls of comatose patients, with the hope that a change of scenery might have some positive effect.

As their research continued, Jane and Amy coined the term *job crafting* to explain what they were seeing. Job crafting means essentially this: that people often take their existing job expectations—or job descriptions—and expand them to suit their desire to make a difference. "We often get trapped into thinking about our job as a list of things to do and a list of responsibilities," says Amy. "But what if you set aside that mindset? If you could adjust what you do, whom would you start talking to, what other tasks would you take on, and whom would you work with?"

In other words, job crafters are those who do what's expected (because it's required) and then find a way to add something new to their work.

Something that delights.

Something that benefits both the giver and the receiver.

Jane told us, "So we started looking at everybody from hospital cleaners to engineers to cooks. Across the whole gambit of different kinds of work, we saw people altering the boundaries of their job descriptions in ways that made their jobs more meaningful."

But what does meaningful mean?

Jane explained, "One of the highs for us, from the research, was to see the importance of other-centered activities. People who job-craft don't just reshape their jobs to make life better for themselves, but to serve others in some beneficial way." This focus on the end result was, and is, quite profound. "As an academic," Jane said, "you are taught motivation theory, which tends to be pretty much based on self-interest. But more and more psychologists are saying, at a basic level, that we may care about self-interest, but we're also very much hardwired to connect with and serve others." It's both.

Creating results that benefit both the "me" and the "we" is at the heart of job crafting. Justin Berg, one of Jane's students who helped with many of her studies, told us, "On average, jobs aren't designed very well for experiencing meaning. First off, they are usually highly bureaucratic and one-size-fits-all. Even the way we communicate jobs is sort of boring and dry. It's just a list of responsibilities in a job description. Meaningful work typically comes from the bottom up, from employees who show initiative through job crafting to kind of put their own take on their job and find opportunities for meaning and satisfaction. Usually those opportunities involve doing things that benefit other people."

How do you see yourself? How do I see myself? Are we defined by our job descriptions? Or is there something more? Something bigger?

In a 2010 paper for the journal *Organization Science*, Justin and some colleagues helped identify several distinct ways in which people craft the jobs they have into more meaningful ones and thereby become more fulfilled and energized. Their findings confirmed what we were seeing in our look at people who had been rewarded for their great work. But one job-crafting technique in particular stood out from all the rest because we'd heard about it in virtually every one of our great work conversations. Justin's team called it *reframing.*

MOSES REFRAMES HIS ROLE

When Ed began to see himself as a marketing consultant with great ideas, rather than as a lowly radio sales rep, he was reframing. Reframing happens when we make a mental connection with a grander purpose of our job: its social benefit, its worth to society, its potential to make a difference. And then we act on that new perception. Thinking of the good our work can do for others, beyond our daily to-do list, helps us change *how* we do what we do in ways that add meaning to our work. Such reframing possibilities exist in practically any occupation. All it takes is a little effort to think beyond our to-do list to those who benefit from our work.

Sometimes the best way to see a difference is through the eyes of the person for whom the difference was made. That's why we talked to Mindi about her family's experience with a hospital janitor in Philadelphia.

It's impossible to imagine the feelings of a parent with a critically ill child. The world stops. You would do anything in your power to make things better.

Mindi and Matt knew that feeling. Their son McKay was born with only half a heart. Instead of four chambers, he had just two. To make matters worse, there was no connection between his heart and his lungs. At birth, McKay needed immediate surgery just to stay alive. Eighteen months and a second surgery later, McKay's skin was consistently blue, and he was on oxygen all the time. But he was getting stronger and growing more rapidly than anyone had expected. Then, just before McKay's third and most critical surgery, tragedy struck. The family's trusted surgeon was diagnosed with a very aggressive cancer. He walked off the job that very day to spend his few remaining months with his family.

After a countrywide search for a new surgeon, Matt and Mindi flew McKay to Philadelphia. McKay made it through the critical lifesaving surgery remarkably well, but the recovery was tough going. "McKay's tiny chest cavity struggled to purge fluid," Mindi explained. "It was 24-hour intensive care." Mindi tried to comfort McKay and get him to rest. But it seemed that the minute he would finally fall asleep, someone would come in to check the incision, to force-feed medicine, or to draw blood. Sometimes one of the janitors in dark blue scrubs would disturb their peace and quiet just to empty the trash. McKay began to whimper every time he heard a knock at the door.

"You quickly learn how to tell who's at your hospital room door by the type of knock," Mindi told us. "Doctors and nurses knock softly and enter quietly. But sometimes really loud, banging knocks would come from custodians." Every time a custodian entered the room, McKay's little lip began to quiver and he looked at his parents in a panic. The custodians would rush toward his bed and grab the trash can. They would make all sorts of noise tidying up the room. Then they would leave McKay and his parents wide awake and frazzled. After the first weekend of these inter-ruptions, Matt and Mindi had had enough. They decided to sit vigil by the door to protect their child from intruders.

The next morning, they heard a soft knock. When Matt opened the door, he and Mindi were surprised to see a very soft-spoken man in dark blue scrubs with a cart. They were confused because they had never heard a custodian knock so quietly before.

He said, "Good morning. My name is Moses, and I'm here to help you welcome the day. Can I come in?" After a quick double take, Matt and Mindi said, "Absolutely."

Instead of rushing forward to empty the garbage can, Moses performed a very small—but significant—act: he stood at the foot of the bed and introduced himself to McKay. "Hi, I'm Moses. I'm here to make things better." It meant a lot to Mindi because it was the first time in four days that someone besides her and Matt had spoken to McKay as a child. To everyone else, he was a patient or a project or a problem. But to Moses, McKay was a person. McKay visibly calmed down. His shoulders relaxed. His lip stopped quivering. Then Moses moved softly, gently to the side of the bed. He picked up the garbage can and emptied it into his cart.

As he began to move around the room doing his job, Moses spoke little wisdoms about light and sunshine and making things clean. He said to McKay, "Moses is here to help. Moses is here to make it all better. You're getting stronger by the minute, aren't you? Got to scrub yesterday out of here. Today is a new day." He gently opened the blinds to let just the right amount of light into the room, then drifted out as quietly as he had come.

From then on, Matt and Mindi and McKay looked forward to Moses' visits twice a day. He became a trusted friend and confidant. When Mindi told a doctor that McKay had played for 10 minutes, the doctor might say, "Very good; let's try for 20 minutes tomorrow." But when she shared the same information with Moses, he would say, "So you went to the playroom, huh? Did McKay walk there by himself? That's good! Once kids start playing, it's not long before they get to go home."

Moses just seemed to understand the family's emotions—because of who he was. He seemed so in tune, and he had such a keen power of observation, that they knew they could trust him. "Doctors seem to rely on all these data we can't see or understand," Mindi said, "all these charts and scans and monitors. But as parents, we're just looking at the simple, outward stuff. Can he sit up? Can he walk? Can he eat yet?" Matt and Mindi would see some small change and think it might be an improvement, but they didn't have the experience of watching hundreds of children in critical care, year in and year out, to know for sure. "We desperately needed the personal confirmation of our son's progress that we got from Moses."

Moses was good at his job. He was efficient. He was always busy making the room clean. But at the same time, he could read the family's emotions. He never made a medical diagnosis or overstepped the bounds of his position. But he shared a lot of practical, commonsense wisdom gleaned from helping hundreds of families make it through traumatic surgery. Moses reinforced the good: "You're sitting up today; that's a good boy." He offered encouragement: "You're brave. You're strong. You can do it." He gave practical advice: "You've been through a lot, but you're coming through it now. Your body knows what to do. Just rest and let it do it."

Matt and Mindi looked forward to visits from Moses because as he made their hospital room clean, he also gave them hope.

As they boarded the plane for their long flight home, McKay was a normal little boy for the very first time in his life. No oxygen tanks. No tubes. Just a regular little two-year-old that the other passengers hoped would stay asleep in his mother's arms. Matt and Mindi were exhausted but grateful as they settled into their seats. Mindi began to make a mental list of people who deserved thank-you notes. They certainly owed one to the surgeon who had saved McKay's life. But Mindi's thoughts went right to Moses. She addressed her first card to him.

Moses was a good janitor. But he also added something extra with his job that made a difference—something outside his job description. He was more than a housekeeper. He made a serious individual contribution to the hospital's mission: to offer hope. He had a higher goal than just keeping rooms clean, and it showed. Moses took his innate talents (his sensitivity) and his practical wisdom (from years of hospital experience) and combined them into a powerful form of patient and family support that changed the critical-care experience for Mindi, Matt, and little McKay.

Mindi told us later, "I think it's the difference between working with your head down and with your head up. You need to look at everything going on around your job so that your eyes are open to possibilities. If you look at how your work affects others, at how relationships work, at what others want and need, you will see things you don't see when you are just going through the motions."

That's what reframing your role is all about: thinking about how your work affects others, looking at the larger purpose of your work and whom it benefits, and seeing yourself as a potential difference maker.

See Mindi share her experience with McKay and Moses in a video by visiting greatwork.com or attending one of our workshops.

CHAPTER 2

WORK WITH
WHAT YOU'VE GOT

GOOD IS THE FOUNDATION OF GREAT.

It's a common notion in the working world today that good is the enemy of great—that embracing good work somehow puts us in danger of never achieving greatness. But the fact is good work has its place—an integral place at that. Good work is proven, understood, stable, tried, true, and tested. A lot of good work needs to get done just to keep our world running smoothly and profitably. Most important, good work is the starting point for adding something great.

Name a truly great product or service. If you look closely, you'll see that great work stands on the shoulders of good work; that the human innovations we love are connected to a historical flux and flow of good into great into good into great over time. That's the rhythm of progress; of change; of innovation. One of the foremost minds of the twentieth-century, Carl Sagan, once said, "If you want to make an apple pie from scratch, you must first create the universe." In other words the apple pie can't come into existence unless the good elements—apples, wheat, cinnamon, sugar—exist in the first place. Thus at the beginning of any great work project, the elements of the task at hand are our friends. Because good is not the enemy of great. Good is the foundation upon which great is created.

In other words, award-winning employees don't invent great work from scratch. Difference making, by its very nature, is the art of taking something good and making it better. It's an act of fine-tuning, improving, and refining, not starting from zero. As comedian Sid Caesar once said, "The guy who invented the first wheel was an idiot. The guy who invented the other three, he was a genius."

We can all be that kind of genius.

Skip Hults didn't take a wrecking ball to Newcomb Central School and construct a smaller building that was better suited to the town's declining population. He started with the good he had—the building, the desks, the chairs, the books, the faculty, the teachers, and the community—and added international students. Ed didn't reinvent his radio station's programming or change its advertising rates. He took what the station had to offer and added food wholesalers as devout customers. Moses didn't stop being a janitor. He added empathy and became a valuable member of the healing team.

It's perfectly natural to feel limited by the constraints of our jobs from time to time. But rather than seeing those constraints as limitations, we can see them as a starting point for making a difference. And when we look at constraints that way, life gets interesting.

As Marty Cooper (one of the *Great Work* interviewees you'll meet later on) told us, "The feeling you get when you do something better than you have to do it is very important to me. If you have an attitude that you are being limited by your environment, then you are being unfair to yourself. People are capable of so much more than what other people expect. The fun that comes from doing something unique and more than what anyone asked you to do ought to encourage everybody."

TED DOES A LOT WITH A LITTLE

Today, writing children's books is the polar opposite of boring, meaningless work. In fact, it's a dream job for many. Consider how many famous people with the freedom to do any job they wish take a crack at writing children's books. Bob Dylan, Steve Martin, Julie Andrews, Billy Crystal, Katie Couric, Justin Bieber, and Barack Obama are just a few of the hundreds of celebrities who've leveraged their fame to become children's book authors.

But this was not always the case.

In the 1950s, children's literature sounded like this: "Look Jane, look! Look at Spot. See Spot run!"

In a 1954 *Life* magazine article titled "Why Johnny Can't Read," author John Hersey pointed out that the "Dick and Jane" books that most schools depended on were just too boring. The books had no real story—just illustrations of children and simple words repeated over and over. To teach reading, they relied on word memorization over phonics (the ability to sound out new words). It wasn't all poor Dick and Jane's fault. Many publishers had their own version of Dick and Jane, including Janet and John, Peter and Jane, Ant and Bee, and Janet and Mark. No kidding. All of these books looked and sounded alike. It was an ocean of sameness. Writing and illustrating these books was no glamorous task.

Write, Janet, write. Write, write, write. Draw, Mark, draw. Draw, draw, draw.

Someone needed to break the mold. To make a difference.

That someone was inspired by William Spaulding, the director of Houghton Mifflin's education division. William read "Why Johnny Can't Read" in *Life* magazine and decided to do something about it. So he took an illustrator friend of his named Ted to dinner and issued a challenge: take 225 unique words that every six-year-old knows and "write me a story that first graders can't put down."

How about those constraints?

Ted was a talented artist with a few children's books in publication. But he had yet to make a big mark on children's literature. At the time, he was better known for a few advertising cartoons he'd done for Ford, NBC, and Standard Oil. But he saw this opportunity to rethink the picture book as something interesting. Something with possibilities. Something worth sinking his time and his heart and his soul into.

At first, Ted thought he could dash off such a book in no time. But as his perfectionism and his desire to make a difference took over, he wrestled with that list of beginner words for a year and a half. Most of the words had only one or two syllables. There weren't many verbs. The task became a mission. Ted embraced the limitations of the list, but he also insisted on creating something great. He said he would come up with a good idea, then find in frustration that the limited word list gave him no way to express that idea. "I read the list three times and almost went out of my head," Ted said, continuing, "I said, 'I'll read it once more, and if I can find two words that rhyme, that will be my book.'"

Luckily, those two words were *cat* and *hat*.

When Ted Geisel (also known as Dr. Seuss) published *The Cat in the Hat* in 1957, children's literature was changed dramatically for the better. It was the first successful book that did not talk down to children. It had wacky illustrations, humor, sarcasm, rhythm, character development, and a story line. There was tension and resolution. The cat challenged authority. The children in the story learned a lesson. It was silly, oddball, and unexpected. It had no soft illustrations of Dick pulling Spot in a wagon and other clichés. Instead, it had a cat in a top hat, a know-it-all scolding fish, and two blue-haired "Things" that made a mess of everything. It was *different*.

And children and parents loved it.

The *New York Times Book Review* said, "Beginning readers and parents who have been helping them through the dreary activities of Dick and Jane and other primer characters are due for a happy surprise." Fueled by playground word of mouth, parents bought enough books to make *The Cat in the Hat* an immediate success. Kids weren't being forced to read the book; they were begging to read it. They were taking it to bed. Millions of copies were sold to families. Schools would soon follow.

The book did more than make Dr. Seuss a household name; it started a revolution in early readers, helped promote phonics as a reading movement to replace rote memorization, and began the slow decline of those dull early readers. Good-bye, Dick and Jane. Hello, Cat.

A lifetime of previous experiences—drawing, reciting rhymes, and creating cartoons—had prepared Ted to reinvent children's literature when that 225-word constraint was set before him. But imagine the loss to the world if Ted had seen William's challenge as just another job with unreasonable constraints that he had to crank out, if his eyes hadn't been open to new possibilities, and if he hadn't had the mindset to make a difference when the opportunity came breezing by.

Five years after the success of *The Cat in the Hat*, another publisher friend bet Dr. Seuss $50 that he couldn't write a successful beginner book with fewer than 50 words. Dr. Seuss took the bet, accepted the challenge, and wrote *Green Eggs and Ham.*

Perhaps we won't all make a difference as far-reaching as that of Dr. Seuss. The point is that there are all kinds of surprising possibilities that come from working with what we've got.

• • •

Architect Frank Gehry, best known for the Guggenheim Museum in Bilbao, Spain, and Disney Concert Hall in Los Angeles, shared how constraints and realities are the building blocks of great work. The strict standards for acoustics at Disney Hall, for example, led to a unique design of the interior space. And that, in turn, led to the soaring, graceful steel exterior that surrounds it. Gehry spoke of how lost he once felt when he was asked to design a house with zero constraints. "I had a horrible time with it," he said. "I had to look in the mirror a lot. Who am I? Why am I doing this? What is this all about?" It's better to have some problem to work on, Gehry explained. "I think we turn those constraints into action."

We love what Gehry is saying, that constraints actually give us some building blocks to work with, a starting point. And without that, nothing happens. If you're ever tempted to feel limited by the constraints of a project, remember how few elements it takes to make something great.

Every color in nature comes from just red, yellow and blue—mixed together in millions of combinations. Every pop song, symphony, jingle, ditty, and aria in the Western World started with just twelve notes in the chromatic scale. Everything on the planet, including us, is made up of just 118 known chemical elements.

Do you know how many building combinations are possible with just six regular eight-stud Lego bricks?

You might do a little elementary math and guess 48 combinations, or perhaps a few thousand. Some might even go crazy and suggest a few hundred thousand. But according to howthingswork.com, six regular eight-stud Lego bricks can be put together in more than 900,000,000 different ways.

How's that for possibilities?

Every one of the people we interviewed for this book found a way to work with what they had to create differences people love. They taught us that we can always find something new to add. There are so many untried combinations, so many avenues to explore, so many ways to shape, enhance, and improve our work. The good news is we don't have to make something from nothing. We get to make something that already exists even better.

Now let's look at the most exciting result of our *Great Work* study: the five skills anyone can use to make a difference people love.

See the mathematics behind the astronomical building possibilities with six Lego bricks at greatwork.com.

WHAT DIFFERENCE MAKERS DO

CHAPTER 3

ASK THE RIGHT QUESTION

GREAT WORK BEGINS WHEN WE TAKE THE TIME TO ASK

IF THERE'S SOMETHING NEW THE WORLD WOULD LOVE.

Albert Einstein said, "If I had an hour to solve a problem and my life depended on it, I would use the first 55 minutes determining the proper question to ask, for once I know the proper question, I could solve the problem in less than five minutes."

In our deep dive into millions of examples of award-winning work, we found a similar starting point. Like Einstein, instead of jumping right in to accomplish whatever task they are assigned, difference makers pause—however briefly or however long it takes—to ask the right question.

And when great work is the objective, that question, while expressed differently by different people, clearly comes down to this, "What would people love?"

Indeed, the lion's share of great work that surprises and delights around the world begins when someone somewhere pauses to consider new ways to delight that may not have been asked for, or thought of, yet. They don't make a big production out of it. They merely stop to think whether an assignment or task that's coming their way might be a great work opportunity in disguise—a chance to create something new, something better, something appreciated by others. This deceptively simple first step sits at the very crossroads of good work and great work.

When one of us gets into a minor traffic accident, our first thought is usually something like, "Oh, great; now I have to deal with my insurance company." But we might be pleasantly surprised if we call our insurance company and get a person who really wants to help. If we're lucky, we may even get someone who learned how to help from Rob.

As the manager of a customer call center at The Hartford, Rob managed a team whose job was processing insurance claims for car accidents. The team dealt with approximately 4,500 claims a month. Navigating those thousands of claims through the gauntlet of customer emotions, government regulations, and company protocol is no easy task. In the insurance world, it's not uncommon for unresolved claims to pile up, employee morale to fade, turnover to escalate, and customer satisfaction to falter. It happens in the best of insurance companies. But it was not acceptable to The Hartford, and it wasn't acceptable to Rob. As manager of a claims department, Rob looked at his less-than-stellar productivity reports and chose to ask the right question: What would his team, his company, and his customers love?

Rob shared with us how he started by asking, "How are we going to get better at this? How can we lower the number of unresolved claims, improve employee morale, stabilize retention, and deliver peace of mind to our customers? How can we get customers back to where they were before their accident as quickly and efficiently as possible?"

One morning, as Rob was mulling over these questions during his morning commute into Phoenix, a story on the radio captured his attention. The talk show host was interviewing a cartographer—someone who draws maps—about the Lewis and Clark expedition. When the cartographer mentioned the Latin phrase *terra incognita* (meaning "unknown land"), it resonated with Rob in a major way. He realized that "unknown land" was exactly what he and his team had been looking for. They needed to look beyond what was already understood about resolving claims to find better ways that were as yet unexplored. "I realized," Rob said, "that as a team, we didn't know what we didn't know. That was the real problem. Our stumbling blocks were familiar territory. The solutions were unknown land."

Later on in *Great Work*, we'll discuss some of the steps that Rob and his team took to create a better insurance claim experience. What's important for the moment is to notice the critical shift in Rob's thinking from work as something familiar to work as unknown land—from just routinely completing the work at hand to pausing to wonder what differences might be loved. We saw exciting evidence of this specific way of thinking in our *Great Work* research. If you were to stack up 100 examples of game-changing work like Rob's—those where someone was delighted by the final result—in 88 of 100 such cases, the creators of the work took the time to consider what people might love.

Rob told us, "From a leadership perspective, there's nothing more frustrating than to see people on autopilot. There's so much more we tap into when we encourage each other to make things better."

THE INTELLIGENCE INSIDE THE PAUSE

It doesn't take any special training to ask the right question. Nor does it require a high IQ. In fact, the only real resource required to ask what people might love is time. Not an eternity—just a moment or two. A pause. Enough time to consider whether something could be done better, faster, or cooler. Most of us are in such a rush just to accomplish things that "good enough" is all we ever shoot for. We'd like to make a difference, but we just don't have the time. Or so it seems.

Jonah and his pals Arielle and Jason were good friends and wannabe entrepreneurs. They hung out regularly to eat, drink, chat, and throw out possible business ideas. On one such occasion, they found themselves joking about the proverbial lonely sock whose mate gets lost in the dryer—a mysterious phenomenon that most of us have experienced. One of them wisecracked, "Why don't we sell socks that don't match?" All three burst out laughing. Then they riffed on to the next topic, ate more, and bantered more. And as the evening wrapped up, they were no closer to a cool business idea than they had been in previous get-togethers.

Except for Jonah.

That night, and for several nights following, he didn't sleep very well. He lay in bed awake, thinking about a lonely sock in search of a mate.

Jonah was in the act of pausing. He took time to listen to his mental cues—his gut feelings, insights, and curiosities. Something about that lone sock kept niggling at him.

He tossed.

He turned.

Ideas hummed.

Possibilities sparked.

And then suddenly he saw her in his mind's eye: a character. A character he would call Little Miss Matched. She would give tween girls permission to be uniquely themselves.

In 2004, Jonah and his friends launched LittleMissMatched Inc. Their first product: a collection of mismatched socks for girls, sold in packs of three with the mantra, "Nothing matches, but anything goes." Today the company has expanded into clothes, accessories, sleepwear, bedding, furniture, books, and more. LittleMissMatched started with a simple vision: "Build a brand that is fun, inspires creativity, embraces individual style, and celebrates self-expression."

What's remarkable about this brilliant business idea is not that it was lobbed out so casually during a friendly conversation, but that Jonah actually paused long enough to listen to the feeling that grabbed hold of him. He considered how young girls might react to the individuality and expression they could get from wearing mismatched socks. He pondered whether that would be something they might love. Even though the great idea he and his friends had been looking for began as a joke, Jonah gave it time to grow. Who knew that a good idea as tried, true, and expected as a pair of identical socks could be tweaked into a great idea of three mismatched ones? That's a powerful example of the intelligence that's available inside the pause.

Just as Jonah lay in bed mulling over the image of a lonely sock, just as Ed drove around in his VW bug thinking of ways to help food brokers move canned goods with radio, just as Skip Hults pondered solutions for his disappearing school in the Adirondacks, just as in every *Great Work* story we've shared up to this point, the difference maker suspends routine just long enough to question the status quo and to develop some initial hunches about what needs improving to make a difference. While good work, crucial as it is, sets our attention on execution and delivery, great work sets our attention on benefiting others. Surely that's worth taking a little time out for.

IT NEVER HURTS TO ASK

Consider the work we all have to do every day. Our plates are certainly full of projects, processes, responsibilities, and deadlines. As good workers, we jump in, forge ahead, aim for completion, and do it all again tomorrow and the next day and the next. This is admirable and necessary. Indeed, the companies we work for require it of us. But these same companies also depend on us to become difference makers.

Thankfully, the world is filled with people who pause to ask. In fact, when you think about it, everything we use in our day-to-day lives—every product, service, or object—began when someone questioned the status quo and wondered what new improvement might be loved. Just scan your environment. Wherever you are, look at the stuff around you. Every single thing, and every part it is made of, was initially made possible because somebody questioned the norm, veered from shopworn thinking, took something as it was, and turned it into something better. Light switches, hair dryers, water fountains, chairs, pillows, toasters, curtain rods, and toothpaste with whiteners all began when someone Asked the Right Question. But the principle doesn't just apply to the physical products around us. Everything else, including valet parking, life insurance, investment banking, yoga, and learning Finnish by immersion, also began with a "How come . . . ?," "What if . . . ?," or "Why can't . . . ?"

If we ask the right question and no great improvements come to mind, there's no harm done. We can always go right back to work as usual with no regrets. The important thing is to not assume that good is good enough, because even good things can always, always find a way to get better. And your unique perspective on what people might love is worth contributing. For one thing, you may find answers that only you can find. For another, if you don't ask the right question, who will?

A CHILD CAN DO IT

It was 1944. The Land family was on vacation in New Mexico, hitting some sights and snapping photos. Three-year-old Jennifer had a question that was really bothering her. As described by her father, Edwin, "I recall a sunny day in Santa Fe, New Mexico, when my little daughter asked why she could not see at once the picture I had just taken of her." Edwin explained to his little girl that the film had to be developed in a special place called a darkroom, and that the negatives had to be printed on special paper. Translated from the perspective of a three-year-old: blah-blah, blah-blah.

We all do this in our own way—explain why things are the way they are to someone who questions the expected—as if the current solution is some foregone conclusion, a done deal. Thank goodness Jennifer was a strong-willed kid who was not satisfied with her dad's answer. She still wanted to know, "Why can't I see my picture right now?" And that sulky disgruntlement got Edwin to thinking: "As I walked around the charming town I undertook the task of solving the puzzle she had set me." Three years later, the camera, the film, and the physical chemistry came together as Edwin and Polaroid introduced the concept of "instant" to the photography world. If you're old enough, you know the rest of the story: the Polaroid Land Camera made photography easy and immediate for everyone; it became a household fixture and remained one for decades. The difference Edwin made soon rippled from home life to work life in the form of ID cards, passport photos, ultrasound pictures, folk art, and police investigations, to name just a few. Even the digital camera in your cell phone, while not invented by Land, carries his fingerprint of "instant."

It's amazing the ideas and opportunities that reveal themselves when we pause to ask the right question. In the case of Edwin Land, in one fortuitous moment, Jennifer's question crossed paths with his know-how, and a difference-making opportunity was born. Edwin was the perfect person to answer little Jennifer's question. An inventor and a self-taught physicist, he knew a thing or two about light and chemistry. Working alongside a group of young scientists, Edwin and his team had already produced the first polarizing light filters for sunglasses, motion picture projectors, and glare-free automobile headlights. In describing the development of the Polaroid camera, Edwin said, "It was as if all that we had done in learning to make polarizers . . . had been a school and a preparation both for the first day in which I suddenly knew how to make a one-step dry photographic process and for the following three years in which we made the very vivid dream a solid reality."

Edwin was uniquely Edwin, that's for sure. When the unexpected called, he seized an opportunity that only someone with his experience and know-how could have seen, grasped, and worked with. That's one of the beauties of being a difference maker.

Difference makers question the norm. They challenge routine and veer from the conventional. They're not so crazy about the idea of "business as usual" because they prefer "business as a means to make something cool." They ask perceptive questions—unusual questions; frank questions; questions that shed light, spark conversation, baffle, bother, and propel. They ask questions that only great work can answer.

Like little Jennifer's wondering why she couldn't see photos right away, questions that lead to great work can seem startlingly obvious. We've all experienced the feeling, "Why didn't I think of that?" (Or, even worse, "Hey, that was my idea.") That just proves we're questioning things all the time, whether we're conscious of it or not. How many times a day do you make mental notes about the things around you—what's mediocre, what's problematic, what's broken, and how you'd do it differently? How many times have you wished you had a dollar, or a patent, or an angel investor for every time you thought to yourself, "There's got to be a better way"?

The truth is, you have this skill nailed. It's only a matter of giving your mental notes their due respect; taking them seriously for a change; tuning in and listening to your own opinions, doubts, and observations. Do so and we can attest: you'll start brimming with fresh thinking, timely solutions, and enthusiasm—all the amazing, inspiring stuff of a difference-making quest.

THREE COMMON STARTING POINTS

In the event that you need a little help Asking the Right Question, we offer three common starting points. These aren't rules or steps. They're more easygoing than that. They're simply ideas to get your great work juices flowing. You can take them, leave them, or invent your own. The point is to have a good time with them—to get curious and playful while wondering what people might love. The ultimate aim of these starting points is to help us think outside the ordinary, to question the conventional way of doing things, and to tune into our hunches about improvements we can make.

Starting Point 1: Tackle a Problem

There's stuff going on all around us that just isn't working quite right: products, processes, and services. Maybe your organization's sales are down, or maybe your customers are dissatisfied. Maybe a team member isn't performing or a procedure isn't working. Whatever it is that's flawed, busted, infuriating, or otherwise counterproductive, take a moment and ask the right question. What would be cooler? Better? More enjoyable? And, perhaps most of all, unexpected? The problems that send our stress through the roof are often loaded with difference-making opportunities. When you begin to see problems as road signs that say "great work possibility; turn here," you're on your way.

Mike had a problem. His company, Shizuki, had built a brand-new state-of-the-art manufacturing plant in Guadalajara, Mexico. In its first two years of operation, the company hadn't been able to hang on to its employees for more than 60 to 90 days. That would be a hair-raising dilemma for any company. But it was particularly unnerving for Shizuki because the new plant had everything an employee could possibly want. The pay was higher than average; the campus was breathtaking inside and out; it provided an in-house cafeteria, a doctor's office on-site, transportation to and from work, a weekly grocery allowance, English classes, karate classes, cooking classes. Compared to other plants in the region (in fact, compared to its own sibling plants in the United States), there wasn't a more desirable place to work. Most of the employees were young women—ages 17 to 22, single, living at home, and helping to support their families. Good jobs were in high demand and were essential to family survival. Yet, like clockwork, every 60 to 90 days the new hires would quit.

Shizuki was in the business of manufacturing tiny capacitors—the energy storage devices that go into just about every electronic device we use. If a speck of dust can destroy a capacitor, you can only imagine what a speck of incompetence could do. Given the high turnover, everything was suffering: production, testing, packaging, shipping, cost, quality, and delivery. Mike, the vice president and general manager at the time, remembers, "The young women weren't staying long enough to get fully trained, to acquire skills, or to master processes. Employees on the floor were always green. Training was a revolving door."

Mike and his team were so stumped about what was broken that they turned to neighboring manufacturing plants in the region, asking if they had been in the same predicament. They had. Their advice was to stick it out, saying that it would take a good eight to nine years to develop a solid employee base. But Shizuki didn't have eight to nine years. The company had to crack the problem or close the plant.

Mike and his team circled the issue for months, trying to figure out how the company was failing these young women. "Is it our managers? Are we handling disagreements poorly? Do we need more perks and benefits? What about better training?" It was baffling and exasperating. Then the team had a moment of insight: "Maybe we're trying to guess at solutions without knowing what's broken in the first place. What if it's not about something we're doing wrong? Maybe there's just something we don't understand about what these young women want from us."

And there it was: the pause to ask the right question.

Sincere as Mike and his team were, they had been mired in old solutions. The moment they decided to try to really understand their employees' needs, everything changed. Suddenly they began to think a little more openly, listen more attentively, and gather new intelligence. The preoccupation with repairing some hypothetical company weakness shifted to a preoccupation with the experience the young women were having at work. What Mike and his team learned was stunning: "Most of those women actually loved their jobs," Mike says. "Some said that working for Shizuki was the best job they'd ever had. The only reason they left again and again was because family duties called them home as soon as they'd made just a little bit of money."

That was a big aha. Shizuki had a turnover issue that all the standard loyalty programs in the world could never have put a dent in. The problem wasn't compensation; it was tradition. Each young woman would work 60 to 90 days. Then, the minute she had a little money, she would quit to return to her duties at home—to help with the washing, cooking, and caring for younger siblings. The pattern would repeat when the family needed money again. For these young women, this was a way of life.

It turned out that Mike and his team were up against a deep-rooted cultural tradition. But by Asking the Right Question, they opened themselves up to all kinds of new possibilities. They tuned into their mental notes, picked a few more brains, and asked around to learn what might possibly influence these young women to say no to going back home after eight weeks on the job.

The answer? A social life.

How's that for obvious?

The young women all said they would stay at work to be near someone they were dating.

On the face of it, that might seem to be outside the realm of work. But not if your work is about doing something people would love. With a bit more digging, Mike and his team learned that the young women at the factory loved dinner dances—music, food, laughter, and mingling with eligible bachelors. The same was true for the guys at the company. They wanted to date more, take their girlfriends out, or meet new girls. But in Guadalajara, dinner dances were expensive.

And there it was.

In a moment of inspiration, Mike and his team decided to host Friday night dinner dances in the company cafeteria. Shizuki had the space, the kitchen, and the chefs. There were musicians on staff who could perform or DJ. The company would invest a couple of hundred bucks in food and hang some decorations. And it would be free for the employees and anyone they wanted to bring along.

The idea was an instant hit. Friday nights went from being a typical night at home with the family or a date night that neither the boys nor the girls could afford to a dinner dance at Shizuki—the "in" place to be, and to be seen, in Guadalajara. The employees loved it. They looked forward to it each week. They talked about it and planned for it. These young people in their teens and twenties flocked to the Shizuki dinner dances to groove, laugh, chat, eat, and make friends. Their new friends didn't replace their family, but they became an important extension of it. The young women now had a reason to stay at the factory beyond just work. Employee retention at Shizuki got an immediate bump and ballooned month by month. The young women began to stay six months, then nine, then eighteen— equal to or greater than any manufacturing plant in Guadalajara.

• • •

The father of modern American shipbuilding, Henry Kaiser, once said, "Problems are only opportunities in work clothes." We'd make that "great work clothes." Problems are crystal balls for difference-making opportunities. They give you a preview of the changes and improvements whose time has come. So embrace what's broken. Set your frustration aside. Whatever the problems are, study them, embrace them, pick them apart, and search for clues. When your aim is great work, problems are indeed only opportunities in work clothes. If you look them straight in the eye, they will inspire the kind of questions that defy the status quo and open your imagination to what's needed next.

Starting Point 2: Consider What You're Good At

Nobody else has your particular background, your experience, skills, smarts, and interests. Job descriptions may come out of a mold, but people do not. You know things; you understand things. You have a history and a work life unlike anyone else's. Respect it. Pay attention to it. Let it inspire curious ponderings and original thinking. There are ways to benefit others that your know-how is perfectly suited for. When you have a feeling that something at work could be improved upon, pay close attention. The door to your own great work quest is about to swing wide open.

Several years ago, a jewelry manufacturer in the United States had a department that needed renovating. Not your everyday dusty remodeling, mind you, but the complete disassembling of a plating room where cyanide, arsenic, and lead had been used to create finishes for cuff links, necklaces, bracelets, rings, and pins.

Given that safer technologies and cleaner processes had become available, everyone welcomed the opportunity to dismantle the plating room. But as a project, it was daunting. It would be a colossal undertaking to get rid of toxic chemicals and equipment in a manner that was 110 percent safe for employees, the company, the community, and the environment. The first bid came in at a shocking $5 million. The second was just under $3 million. Both of the toxic cleanup companies consulted were unwilling to do the entire project from beginning to end, and both of them included conditions that would hamper the company's day-to-day operations. What to do? The costs were astronomical, as was the inconvenience. Most gravely, could these cleanup companies be trusted to do the job safely?

Enter an unassuming manager named Annette. As the numbers came in and project details began to materialize, Annette told us she just had a feeling. And her feeling said, "I think we could save the company money and keep people safer if we did this work ourselves." Because of the project's complexity, no one else had even considered the idea. But Annette trusted what she knew. As manager of refinery and environmental compliance, she trusted her own rare background and experience. And in so doing, she transformed an ordinary work assignment into a great work possibility.

Unbeknownst to the company's leaders, people with the ideal background, experience, skills, and smarts to handle the cleanup were within the walls of the company all along. Annette and her coworkers had all been trained for toxic cleanup. Ten years on the spill team had prepared them with specialized knowledge and skills. Add to that Annette's personal history and expertise: "I was raised on a farm in Eastern Colorado with nine brothers and sisters," Annette explained. "Nothing was ever wasted. Everything was repurposed. When it came to my work ethic, my mother, who was a nurse, taught me to always give more to my employer than I was paid." Later on, Annette got her degree in engineering, ultimately working on a rescue team in a New Mexico coal mine. Annette explained, "Safety was drilled into me for an entire year of training. I was taught every feasible danger—how to avoid it and how to respond if something terrible should happen." When you look at Annette's life history—farm-inspired sustainability plus work ethic plus safety—it's obvious that she was prepared to ask the right question: wouldn't it be good for the company and for everyone's safety if we could do this cleanup for ourselves?

The green light didn't come instantly, of course. Annette and her team, along with numerous company executives, studied the project for months. They connected with the Occupational Safety and Health Administration (OSHA) and the Environmental Protection Agency (EPA). They talked to numerous laboratories on testing protocols. They spoke with the crews in New York City who cleaned up after 9/11. They even worked with the Department of Housing and Urban Development to establish protocols so rigorous that babies would be safe in the renovated area. Every moment would be recorded on camera. Every *i* would be dotted and every *t* crossed. It had to be done perfectly. The smallest slip could be disastrous.

But Annette says, "I just had this nagging feeling that the company was being taken advantage of by the bids that were coming in. I knew we could do it. It felt like a great opportunity. It felt exciting from the very beginning. Management thought twice and a third time and a fourth time, and every time it solidified in my heart that we could do it."

For three grueling months, Annette and her team worked overtime to painstakingly disassemble the plating room and destroy all toxic chemicals and equipment. The final cost to the company was $109,871, a savings of millions. More important was the safety issue. Annette and her team understood that no one outside the company would feel as intimately accountable as she and her team would. They were driven to make certain that every single item coming out of the plating department was safe before it was disposed of. Not kind of safe, not mostly safe, but totally safe.

That's the thing about deciding that we want to make a difference for others. Our work becomes incredibly personal. Ordinary is no longer an option because we are bringing our own history and know-how to the work itself. It reflects a piece of us. And we have the ability to insist on doing something great—something people will love and appreciate.

When everything was completed, the Workers Compensation Fund assessed the renovated area. They found that every detail had been done by the book and beyond. Not a single hazardous mistake had been made. Annette's willingness to ask the right question had set the course coordinates for a toxin-free plating area and kept everybody on track throughout the journey. "The whole point of great work," explained Annette, "is to put your heart and soul into something. Not because you were told to, but because you want to do something that makes a difference."

The truth is, when we see ourselves as a box on somebody's org chart, we're miscalculating our own potential. When we tune into our particular know-how—our history, skills, talents, and curiosities—we access our own specialized brand of intelligence. The late Martha Graham, a modern dancer and pioneer in the performing arts, said, "There is a vitality, a life force, an energy, a quickening that is translated through you into action, and because there is only one of you in all of time, this expression is unique. And if you block it, it will never exist through any other medium and it will be lost. The world will not have it."

The message here is important: there are ingenious questions and hunches that only you will think of. So tune into your history, your experience, and your inimitable take on things. If you've got a nagging feeling that there's a better way, pay attention. Give your smarts a listen. You know stuff. And what you know is all you need in order to ask questions that no one else has thought to ask.

Starting Point 3: Think Out on the Edge

There are some brilliant and enterprising ideas out there on the fringe of possibility. They express themselves in the form of crazy notions, wacky thoughts, impossible dreams. But these free-spirited voices often turn out to be nuggets of genius in disguise. If we tune in and listen to them, they may turn our concept of work inside out and upside down. They'll thrill us. They'll perplex us. They may even scare us a little. But they can also guide us to the great work we are destined to do.

Out of the 7 billion people on the planet, about 5 billion benefit from Marty's pause to ask the right question—and not just occasionally, but literally countless times in countless ways every single day. We inter-viewed Marty and found out he asked a question that was so far beyond what was expected, so far out, so off-kilter that it set his team on a trajec-tory that would transform the very way the world communicates.

In the early 1970s, Martin Cooper was an electrical engineer at a com-pany called Motorola. It may be renowned today for its leading-edge tech-nology, but when Marty was hired in 1954, Motorola was a small company competing in the shadow of the technological juggernaut AT&T.

Marty spent the first 15 years of his career developing various tech-nologies for personal communication—pagers for doctors, crystals for wristwatches, and the first portable handheld police radios, to name a few. Like all of us, he grew into his ingenuity—his natural ability to listen to his hunches and think a little off-center.

By the early 1970s, Marty had risen through the ranks to assume the title of general manager of Motorola's Communications Systems Divi-sion. Given his years of experience developing portable communica-tions, Motorola put him in charge of developing the next-generation car phone. The accepted notion at the time was that moving the phone from the home or office to the car would make people way more accessible.

But Marty didn't just jump right in and do the task he had been assigned. He paused. He took time to listen to a crazy hunch. "People want to talk to people—not a house, an office, or a car," he thought. This led to a status-quo-challenging question as profound as little Jennifer Land's question about instant photography: "Why is it that when I want to call a person, I have to call a place?"

Marty and his team spent the next few years developing the very first handheld cellular telephone. On April 3, 1973, Marty made the world's first mobile call from a 2½-pound cell phone that his team lovingly called "the brick." It had a battery life of 20 minutes. "The battery life didn't matter much," Marty says, "because you couldn't hold the phone up for that long."

It's important to note that Marty and his team were assigned to develop the car phone. They could easily have rushed ahead and done just that. But Marty had a crazy idea, a cockeyed hunch, that what people would love even more than a car phone would be the ability to call anyone, anywhere. So he Asked the Right Question and delivered more. He certainly could have stayed within the constraints of Motorola's assignment. He could have even made some improvements, like making the car phone's cord retractable or integrating the phone with the car's speaker system. But the phone would have still been tethered to a car. His off-kilter idea removed the car from the equation altogether.

The brilliance of Marty's hunch is not just that it reoriented the project's direction, but that it totally reinvented it. Think about the difference Marty's improvement made: the ability to reach one another whenever and wherever; to network and share our lives in small circles and global circles; to take pictures, share videos, and listen to music; to schedule appointments, text, and e-mail; to access just about every whim or interest via custom apps—it has all been made possible because 40 years ago a relatively unknown Motorola engineer chose to Ask the Right Question. Marty's work affected many more people than the average great work project. But our look at award-winning employees has revealed that pausing to Ask the Right Question, just as Marty did, makes our work 313 percent more likely to be considered important by others and increases the likelihood of our work having an impact on two or more people by as much as 412 percent.

When we interviewed Marty for this book, we were struck by the irony that the interview itself would not have been possible without Marty's great work. He was in a waiting room somewhere, talking to us on a cell phone.

It's probably tempting to read Marty's story and think of him as a visionary genius. But if we rewind history 40 years, Marty, like most of us, was just a regular person in a regular job with regular expectations. No one knew in those days that Marty's question, and the great work that followed, would create the cell phone, nor that the cell phone would shape-shift into the handheld computer it is today. Not even Marty. What makes Marty's story inspiring was his ability to pause and listen to the intelligence out on the fringe—to imagine the farfetched, to think a little harebrained, to gut check what would knock people's socks off, and ultimately to believe in his own crazy hunch.

Crazy but brilliant ideas are inside of all of us if we allow ourselves to pause and listen. If you've seen the 1995 movie *Babe*, you know it's about a piglet who dreams of being a sheepdog. Babe's owner, Farmer Hoggett, has a hunch that the little piglet can do it. Writers George Miller and Dick King-Smith characterized perfectly the value of listening to hunches with this line from the narrator: "Farmer Hoggett knew that little ideas that tickled and nagged and refused to go away should never be ignored, for in them lie the seeds of destiny."

We've all got crazy ideas that tickle and nag. Let's turn up the volume on these great work muses. Allow them to germinate, mature, and grow.

Listen to what's quirky and off-kilter. Embrace what seems unfeasible. These inspired voices on the fringe can transform our good work into great work. They can guide us to our own perceptive questions, imaginative hunches, and difference-making opportunities.

?

When early scholars wrote in Latin, they would use the word *quaestiō* at the end of a sentence to signal that it was a query. That took up too much space. So in the Middle Ages, *quaestiō* got abridged to *qo*, with the *q* appearing above the *o*. Then, over time, natural refinements shaped that stacked *q* and *o* into the well-known squiggle and dot that we use today. It's a fitting symbol for all the curious hunches of a difference-making quest. Each is a journey that's oriented and navigated, from departure to destination, by the question mark itself.

quaestio   qo   q̊   q̥   ?

Evolution of the question mark

But Asking the Right Question is just the first step in becoming a difference maker. A useful phrase from the days of Aristotle says, "Nature abhors a vacuum." In not-too-scientific terms, that means that when there's an empty space, nature will attempt to fill it. Think how air rushes to fill the void when you open a vacuum-sealed jar. Asking the

Right Question creates a sort of empty space in the brain for new ideas. That, in turn, allows all kinds of possibilities, refinements, and improvements to start rushing in.

Once we set our intention on making a difference for others, we're ready to start looking for new ideas and possibilities.

QUICK TAKE: HOW TO MASTER THIS SKILL

? ASK THE RIGHT QUESTION

Take the time to ask what people might love.
- Pause as a project begins or schedule time weekly.
- Think about the people your work serves.
- Consider customers, team members, leaders, and partners.
- Ponder improvements with the recipients in mind.
- Can you make something easier? Simpler? Faster? Safer? Greener? Smarter?
- Can you make it more affordable? More convenient? More enjoyable? More connected? Or more secure?

Tackle a problem.
- Pay attention to processes, products, or services.
- Turn problems into opportunities.
- Think small. Think big.

Consider what you're good at.
- Respect your hunches about what people would love.
- Trust your history to help you see possibilities that others might miss.
- If there's a task you enjoy, start there.

Think out on the edge.
- Entertain crazy notions that lead to brilliant ideas.
- Imagine what people might love if anything was possible.

CHAPTER 4

SEE FOR YOURSELF

DIFFERENCE MAKERS LOOK WITH THEIR OWN EYES
FROM A VARIETY OF PERSPECTIVES TO SEE NEW POSSIBILITIES.

It's amazing how many different ways people look at their work and everything that touches it in order to answer that all-important question, "What would people love?"

Every day, in millions of jobs, actively seeing work from new points of view helps people answer questions like: "What's being done now?" "What's missing?" and "How can we make it better?" Seeing for Ourselves is about looking for difference-making opportunities that others might have missed. It's just as useful for daily tasks as it is for major innovations. It's as necessary for entry level employees as it is for CEOs. It's not only highly accessible and feasible for everybody, but also fun and habit forming, because seeing new possibilities for ourselves is easy—once we decide to look.

In a twist of fate, the importance of looking came to us as we ourselves looked at people who do great work. As we met with and interviewed hundreds of people, we saw and heard over and over that something mystical and, dare we say, visionary occurs when people go looking for ways to delight others. Inevitably, the mere act of looking causes possibilities that no one has seen before to come out of the woodwork—not immediately, but in time. As people get better and better at looking, the volume of new possibilities flows with ever-increasing intensity.

As we looked at the records of thousands of employees who were given awards for doing great work, we found that people who go looking for ways to make improvements are 17.1 times more likely to feel passion for their work than those who do not. Isn't that interesting? Something happens to us when we See for Ourselves. It awakens our passion for making a difference. And whenever bottom-line results were mentioned as being among the reasons that an award was given (that is, the great work either made or saved money), 87 percent of the time, the manager said the employees had looked at their work in a new way—to see what might be loved, to see how things work, or to seek new solutions.

Management consultants often misquote hockey legend Wayne Gretsky as having uttered this seemingly visionary phrase: "Skate to where the puck is going, not where it has been." That's a rather over-quoted rallying cry for visionary thinkers. But there's a backstory to the Gretsky quote that's seldom told. First, it was actually Wayne's father, Walter, who coined that phrase. Whenever Wayne said it, he was quoting dear old dad. Second, as a young boy growing up in Canada, Wayne Gretsky used to watch hockey games on television in a rather astounding way. He would begin by drawing a hockey rink on a piece of paper. Then he sat, pencil in hand, and drew lines that followed the direction of the puck. He looked at and recorded everywhere the puck went. Around and around the rink. Passes here. Shots there. Deflections off the wall. This wasn't easy. It demanded his full attention (not to mention a bit of hand-eye coordination). At the end of each game, his paper rink would be covered with pencil lines. There would be white spaces here and there, but much of the page would be covered with lines. One day, Wayne's father asked him what on earth he was doing. He simply held up the paper and said, "Can't you see, Dad? Where all the lines cross, that's where the puck is most of the time."

That story, more than any visionary catchphrase, teaches us the art of seeing future great work opportunities. Wayne Gretsky *did* seem to have an uncanny knack for knowing where the puck was going to be. But that was due, at least in part, to one simple fact: *he had looked*.

YOU SEE TOMATO. I SEE TOMATO

The iris structure of the human eye is so unique that no two eyes are exactly alike. Not the eyes of identical twins. Not even the two eyes of the same person. That's why iris identification is being widely adopted, alongside fingerprinting, as a method of telling who is who.

But what matters when it comes to great work is not how different our eyes appear to be, but how differently they see. Each of us has a unique perspective on the world around us, an inner eye that has more to do with how we *think* than with what we *see*. It's based on many things: our collective experiences, hopes, dreams, fears, loves, hates, choices, talents, abilities, interests, and more.

This brings us to a singular and important reason for Seeing for Yourself: because you will see things that no one else can see.

In June of 2007, a man named Jack hiked a red-rock bluff above the small farming community of Heber, Utah. The bluff included a few dry gullies, some scrub oak, and a beautiful view of the Heber Valley and Wasatch Mountains beyond. But Jack could see something that you and I could not: a fairway here, a dogleg there, a tricky downhill par three off a red-rock cliff—an entire course layout for Red Ledges that *Golf* magazine would name the No. 1 Best New Private Golf Course in 2009. While Jack reminds us that course designs are "the collaboration of a talented team," every course he designs is inspired by what he *sees* in his mind's eye during that first walk of the terrain. And what Jack sees is directly related to the fact that his last name is Nicklaus.

With his record of 18 major golf championships, Jack is arguably the best golfer ever. When he walks a bare patch of land, he brings an entire memory bank of experiences with him: thousands and thousands of shots on courses in places like Scotland, Arizona, Hawaii, and Fiji. Jack has a lifetime of experiences that affect his great work. And so do all of us.

We each have our own history of learning and growing and developing skills. These experiences qualify each of us to view the world through a special lens called [*your name here*]. It's a one-of-a-kind perspective that allows us to see improvements that no one else can see and do great work that no one else can do. It makes you wonder, doesn't it? What great work did your life's experiences prepare you to see? What does your team, your company, and the world need you, and only you, to contribute? What great work will go undone if you don't do it?

There are many ways for us to See for Ourselves. We can read books, pore over reports, watch online videos, study similar products or processes, or Google stuff. But the most juicy, insightful, and irreplaceable way to See for Yourself is to be there. In person. Scientists call it fieldwork. Artists call it leaving the studio. Business leaders call it Management by Walking Around. College students call it a road trip. Call it what you will, it's about getting up off your chair, going where the action is, and seeing things firsthand. Because when we see things for ourselves, with our own two eyes, it changes us. When we experience a problem or watch a customer interact with our work, it becomes almost impossible for us not to care, to take ownership, to look to improve and delight in any way we can.

Since there are as many ways of looking as there are people and projects, we'll share just six of the many ways in which people See for Themselves. You may feel inspired to go looking in these specific ways, or you may find your own way of Seeing for Yourself.

IDEO Looks at People

A few years ago, we made a visit to a top innovation and design firm, IDEO. The people who work there aren't household names, but the products they design are. IDEO designers have worked on everything from the very first Apple mouse to the Swiffer Sweeper. For anyone whose work even remotely touches product development, a trip to IDEO is like a pilgrimage. We couldn't wait to see how these people do what they do.

So we arrived in Palo Alto, and the people at IDEO escorted us around their campus. It was 70 degrees in the middle of winter. Gorgeous. The doors and windows were open. There was a certain cool factor. You could just feel the energy, the buzz, and the caffeine. There was an old VW bus in the building that they used as a conference room. And there were interesting products everywhere. We came around one corner and saw this amazing high-tech baby stroller. It didn't look like the flimsy strollers of a few years earlier. It had big wheels. The seat was high off the ground. There was a big storage area underneath. It just *looked* completely different from the generations of strollers that had come before.

It turns out that IDEO had been engaged to design a new stroller for Evenflo. If you think about it, strollers have been around for a long time. One might expect that after a few decades, the stroller would have been pretty much innovated out. But the IDEO designers began the stroller project with their eyes and minds wide open. They made no assumptions. Then they went out to See for Themselves. When we say they went out to see, we mean that they fully encountered the project from every possible angle. They observed the traditional stroller in all its aspects: its quirks, its purpose, its parts, its materials, its users, and really everything that surrounds it or touches it. They wondered, "What are the intentional and unintentional consequences of a stroller's design?"

But they did more than Ask the Right Question. They left their hip offices to go looking for answers. They visited parks and shopping malls. They brought cameras and took still photos and videos of people and their strollers. They looked intently, with curiosity and purpose. They were determined to discover new possibilities for improvement—new ways to delight. And as they looked, they clearly saw ideas for a better stroller that no one had seen before. They kept notes and connected new ideas to everything they saw.

When they came back, they posted all their photos on a wall with little thought bubbles, sketches, and all kinds of random notes and ideas— lots of ideas. You could practically feel the gears turning. Looking at that wall, you got the notion that somebody had really looked at and paid attention to how people interact with strollers, maybe for the first time, and called things out. It was deep. It was rich. It was substantive. We could have looked at that wall for an hour and not taken it all in. There were people with strollers in every possible situation: getting out of a car; trying to fold a stroller while holding a baby; bending over to play with a baby in a stroller; holding a cup of coffee in one hand and pushing the stroller with the other; putting a kid in a stroller for a nap. There were hundreds of new perspectives, each one an aha for the design team.

We had never seen anything like it before.

Apple founder Steve Jobs explained the importance of Seeing for Yourself when he said, "Design is a funny word. Some people think design means how it looks. But of course, if you dig deeper, it's really how it works. . . . To design something really well, you have to get it. . . . It takes a passionate commitment to really thoroughly understand something, chew it up, not just quickly swallow it. Most people don't take the time to do that." And, to underscore the value of seeing for yourself, rather than asking people what they would love, Steve also said, "A lot of times, people don't know what they want until you show it to them."

The number one reason for looking more purposefully at our work is so that we can really understand and see possibilities for improvement that don't exist yet. The truth is, we can't see what we aren't looking at.

The stroller design team looked hard to understand strollers and the people who use them. Our host took us through some of the specific results of looking and the improvements they inspired. As you look at them, notice how each observation led directly to an improvement. Each new observation became a new innovation—a step forward from the way strollers had been designed for decades.

- Because they saw people struggling to get strollers over cracks in the sidewalk, they made the wheels bigger.
- Because they saw people trying to collapse and uncollapse the stroller while holding a baby, they made it fold and unfold with just one hand.
- Because they saw mothers leaning over to tend to their children, they made the seat higher.
- Because they saw dads struggling to keep children happy with rattles and toys, they made a play area for the baby.
- Because they saw mothers bundling their babies in blankets, they made the stroller soft, enveloping, stable, and safe.
- Because they saw dads juggling grocery bags, diaper bags, and coffee cups, they added storage underneath the baby and cup holders above.

Clearly, each observation the team made brought new value. It gave the designers a repository of great ideas to play with—things they could add to or remove from the original product to create a difference people would love. Indeed, when the strollers hit the market, people loved them. The world accepted them as great work. As proof, several years later, almost every stroller on the market, regardless of the manufacturer, has copied ideas from the Evenflo stroller.

In hindsight, the process of looking for new ways to improve the stroller seems almost too easy. But if it was so easy, why had no one thought to do it before? There's the epiphany. As we said earlier, great work is notorious for causing the familiar reaction: "Why didn't I think of that?" We can't help but wonder: Did it take a visionary to see the possibilities for a better stroller? Or could anyone with the right skills have done it? The reality is, Seeing for Yourself isn't some extremely rare talent. It's simply a skill—and a choice. Anyone can choose to look. And like any other skill, the more we practice, the better we can see.

Jim Looks at the Process

We believe that if an idea has the potential to delight others, it's probably worth pursuing. But even worthwhile improvements come with problems baked in: challenges, objections, and speed bumps. And that's where looking at processes can help. It's fascinating how many things only *seem* impossible until someone has a good look and finds a way.

Back in 1997, Jim and a few partners had a hunch that people might love to rent DVDs via the Internet and have them delivered to their homes by mail. But the idea had a few problems. Some said that mailing would be too expensive. Others said that the DVDs would get lost or stolen. Most agreed that DVDs would never survive multiple mailings back and forth to multiple viewers without becoming damaged in transport.

Rather than relying on conjecture, Jim went to See for Himself. "We knew that if we didn't find a way to work within the U.S. Post Office's systems, we wouldn't succeed," he says. "To understand how the Post Office backend worked, I spent hundreds of hours at a few of the largest regional Postal Centers, observing and asking questions. I noticed letters being sorted by several high-speed spinning circular drums. While these crushing metal drums enabled the separation and processing of over 40,000 standard-size letters per hour, it was obvious a thin plastic

DVD would not survive the journey. With a sinking stomach, I felt the business idea slip away."

Jim could have stopped right there. Luckily he kept right on looking for himself. He continues, "But then I noticed a separate conveyor belt sorting magazines and other larger pieces of 'flat mail.' How would I ensure our package always used this flat mail machine and not the letter sorter? I found out that if an envelope had certain dimensions and other characteristics, it would be sorted by this alternate system instead of the large, crushing metal drums. Better yet, this flat mail sorting machine would read a bar coded delivery address and could automatically sort the item into 'carrier walking route' sequence. Now the wheels were really turning. . . . Our resulting 'Netflix envelope' was one of our biggest 'customer wows.' Its design was critical not only for the customer experience but also for our operations and business model."

For Jim, as a cofounder of Netflix, that deep look at Post Office processes and procedures proved to be worth millions. In fact, within a few years, that business idea would put many video rental stores out of business.

Jim's meticulous look at mail-sorting methods reminds us that there's no good substitute for Seeing for Yourself to understand how things work, troubleshoot problems, and create a path for the improvements we want to make. In fact, there are very few improvements we can make if we are working blind. Understanding requires our own observation. Solutions frequently come in the form of mental pictures. The only prescription is to get out and use our eyes to see how things work. With practice, we'll start seeing paths to improvements that we want to make everywhere—even in the most unexpected places.

Eiji Looks at Nature

Sometimes Seeing for Ourselves means looking outside of things that are obviously connected to our work—looking at things like art or literature or the natural world around us. We discovered this in a dramatic way when we talked to a mild-mannered Japanese engineer named Eiji Nakatsu.

The bullet trains that run between Osaka and Hakata, Japan, are among the fastest trains in the world. They transport commuters comfortably and quietly at 300 km/h (186 mph). If one of these trains passed you when you were doing 90 in your car, you'd feel like you were standing still. But when the trains were first tested, there was a serious problem: tunnel booms were rattling neighborhoods.

Eiji told us, "About half of the entire Sanyo Shinkansen line is made up of tunnel sections. When a train rushes into a narrow tunnel at high speed, this generates atmospheric pressure waves that gradually grow into waves like tidal waves." When test trains exited the tunnels, pressure waves traveling at the speed of sound made a boom that people could feel up to a quarter of a mile away. It was an unpleasant experience for neighbors near the tunnels and wildlife in the area. First, the engineers looked at widening the tunnels, but that was cost prohibitive and not an option. Eiji and his team needed to solve the problem by changing the design of the trains themselves. But how?

One engineer decided to see for himself by riding on a test train. He said it felt as if the cars were all being pushed together as the train rushed into a tunnel. Eiji saw immediately, "This must be due to a sudden change in air resistance." This led him to a very important place to go looking. He asked, "Can we find some living thing that manages sudden changes in air resistance as a part of daily life?"

Now is a good time to mention that, in addition to being an engineer, Eiji is also an active member of the Wild Bird Society of Japan.

He's a bird-watcher.

As Eiji looked to nature, he thought of the kingfisher. He had seen these brightly colored birds barely make a splash as they dove from the air into the water to catch small fish. He looked at the kingfisher and wondered: if a kingfisher's shape allows it to cross from the low resistance of air to the high resistance of water at such great speed, perhaps it holds the key to trains rushing quietly through tunnels as well.

Eiji informed the members of the design team of the kingfisher's beak profile. They, in parallel, conducted simulation tests of trains with different front ends running through tunnels using a research supercomputer. Over time, as they looked at design after design, the solution created through detailed analysis by the supercomputer began to look more and more like the beak of a kingfisher.

It's a bird. It's a train.

Today, the tapered 49-foot nose of the 500-series Shinkansen train looks uncannily like the beak of the bird that inspired it. The design reduced air pressure by 30 percent, decreased electricity use by 15 percent, and even increased speed by 10 percent. And, of course, these trains run at top speed completely free from tunnel booms.

"I tell all our younger engineers to carefully observe nature," Eiji says, "I myself have learned a lot from watching birds. But true inspiration comes from building up a stockpile of observations over many years." Eiji left us with a quote from a book he loves, *Aircraft Designing Theory* by Masao Yamana and Hiroshi Nakaguchi, "A tree, a blade of grass, a bird or a fish, all can be brilliant and everlasting teachers."

Denise Looks at Every Last Detail

We talked to many difference makers who look at every last detail to understand their projects inside and out. They stand shoulder to shoulder with factory workers on assembly lines, watch people do their laundry at home, make trips to suppliers, keep watch on the competition, and perform hundreds of other variations of Seeing for Themselves, because each new perspective adds critical information, new ideas, and fuel for the difference-making journey.

Picture the amount of garbage from your own household that you wheel to the curb each week. For most of us, it's at least a trash can full. Now imagine being told that you can't send anything to the landfill anymore. We're not talking about a little reduction here. You can never throw anything away. Never.

Not long ago, we made a trip to visit Denise Coogan of Subaru of Indiana. Her story begins in 2002. As Denise sat in a semiannual meeting with executives from Subaru's parent company, Fuji Heavy Industries, she got a bit of a shock. "I was basically sitting in this meeting, just getting used to all the Japanese-English translation and trying to follow along," she told us, "and all of a sudden they are saying they'd like us to do all we can to head toward zero landfill by 2006. As manager of safety and environmental compliance, I'm nodding my head 'yes,' but totally not realizing what I'm saying yes to. I left there thinking, 'Uh-oh, what did I just do?'"

Subaru of Indiana is a mammoth car factory—3.8 million square feet, the equivalent of six-and-a-half football fields, under one roof. Giant rolls of steel and other raw and partially finished materials go in one end. Every two minutes, a finished automobile drives out the other end. How could such an operation produce no waste at all? Denise remembered reading about zero landfill initiatives in the 1990s and thinking, "That's impossible. You simply have to send *something* to a landfill. How could you ever not?" From her perspective, Denise and her team were faced with having to do the impossible.

However, as the opportunity to be a part of something cool began to sink in, Denise and her team thought, "Wow, we have no idea where to even begin. Let's just start Dumpster diving and go from there."

Team by team, station by station, they started dumping trash carts and containers on the floor and sorting everything into piles, just to look at what they were dealing with. They made piles of plastics, steel, Styrofoam, cardboard, pallets, and everything else, and weighed them. With those preliminary weights in hand, they could calculate, for each car produced, how much of each commodity they were producing as land-fill. It didn't look good. Even though Subaru had always been an environmentally conscious company, the plant was generating 49 pounds of waste for every car it made. At 600 cars a day, that meant it was sending just under 30,000 pounds, or about 15 tons, of waste to the landfill every 24 hours.

You don't just make 15 tons of waste per day disappear. Or do you?

Little by little, the team members began looking for new places for all that junk to go. "Waste is just a material that hasn't found its use yet," Denise said. "So, between shifts, we started turning over containers and looking at our processes very keenly; giving everything a real laser look. Because our associates have such an intimate knowledge of their own tasks, we asked them to look and see what they could do to reduce some of this waste."

Pretty soon, the suggestions started to flow.

"Recycling is really at the very bottom of our list," Denise said. "First, we have to ask, 'Do we really need this thing?' And that's key. Because if we can simply stop something from coming into the plant in the first place, it's off our list." So they began to look at things like cardboard containers, where they could ask suppliers to ship in reusable containers instead. That made one small difference. Obviously, less cardboard coming in means less going out. However, the biggest waste item was steel. So the team looked at how the cars were stamped or cut from large metal sheets known as blanks. Imagine using a cookie cutter on dough and you get the general idea. Solutions didn't come immediately, but the team ultimately found a way to save steel by using the very outer edges of the blanks, cutting every last inch of steel into a usable part. Again, less steel was coming in and less was going out. Similarly, welding machines have copper tips that need to be replaced when they get dull. So the Subaru machine shop created a sharpener for the tips. Now, by sharpening and reusing the tips, they buy a few hundred tips a month instead of a few thousand. Sure, the copper shavings and tips that are too small to sharpen get recycled. But the most important step was to stop buying so many tips in the first place.

"If we can't eliminate something," Denise explained, "the next option is to find some way to reuse it." That means looking around for new uses for stuff. Department by department, scrap by scrap, Denise and her team looked for themselves at what they had and decided whether it could be reused. Oak and pine pallets got tossed back on trucks and sent back to suppliers for multiple trips, serving a purpose instead of being thrown away. Styrofoam containers for spark plugs, once thought too fragile to be used more than once, have now crossed the ocean up to 20 times to be alternately emptied, filled, and emptied again. When car joints are sealed to keep water out, the excess sealer used to be scraped off and thrown away. Now it's saved, placed back in a bucket, and used on the next car. Not a bit gets thrown out.

Whatever can't be eliminated or reused still has to go somewhere, and that's where recycling comes in. "We got a baler so that any cardboard we can't get rid of altogether gets compacted into blocks that can be stacked and sent for recycling," Denise explained. "The pallets we can't reuse get sent off and chipped up for garden mulch. We looked far and wide for partners who can recycle as many different waste products as possible. We have a partner, Heritage Interactive, that helps us find recyclers for everything from plastic caps to steel shavings to paper products. Food waste from our cafeteria and the biodegradable plates and napkins we use don't go out for recycling. They are composted here on site, and our associates take home really great compost for their gardens."

Since Denise and her team started looking for ways to reduce, reuse, and recycle, the 49 pounds of waste generated per car has been reduced to just 0.07 pound—and even that doesn't get sent to the landfill. It goes to a partner, Covanta Energy, where it gets burned to generate the steam that spins the giant turbines that help power downtown Indianapolis.

"People are always asking me to describe some big project or single initiative that made a difference," Denise said, "but it didn't happen that way. Things never happen all at once or in giant steps. It's really the result of thousands of little projects, one at a time. It's not about what you do in a year but about what you do each week. It's really true that the little things add up."

On May 4, 2004, a year and a half before the deadline to get as close as possible to zero landfill, Denise's team sent a final load of filter cake from Subaru of Indiana's wastewater facility to the landfill. While getting the paperwork together, Denise and her associates realized, "This is it. This is the very last time we're going to have to do this." At first, they couldn't believe that their landfill days were over. So they waited. Week after week ticked by, and nothing needed to be sent to the landfill. Not a scrap. Everything was now either reduced, reused, or recycled in some way. So, they decided to announce to their supervisor, their associates, and the world that Subaru of Indiana was a zero-landfill facility; a car manufacturing plant as large as a small city, full of machinery, people, and raw materials and producing 600 cars a day, was sending less garbage to the curb each week than your family does.

Denise is quick to point out that her achievement was a team effort. "Once we got 3,700 people involved and excited about zero landfill, their synergy was key to our success. I'm a firm believer that 99 percent of the people that walk into a workplace want to do a good job. Our employees embraced the program and made it their own. They take a great deal of pride in it. Everyone gets a real high from doing something this important."

The differences made are astounding. Aside from all those tons of waste *not* going to the landfill, Subaru of Indiana has actually made money by going landfill free. Denise explained, "You take into account the costs of the program—our bean counters have every nickel of that accounted for—and over the last five years we have enjoyed a $10 million benefit. Waste is money, and when you're bringing in steel you don't need, cardboard you don't need, and all these other things you don't need, you're having to pay to bring them in, pay to handle them while they're here, and then pay to throw them away. So when people say, 'It costs too much to be environmentally friendly,' we say, 'No, it costs too much *not* to be environmentally friendly.'"

Could Denise and her team have accomplished their goals working blind? Could they have seen thousands of small ways to reduce, reuse, and recycle without looking at every plastic and metal scrap from a new point of view? We don't think so.

Denise and her team looked everywhere and discovered solutions to problems that were there for the seeing. But Seeing for Ourselves doesn't just make great work possible. It makes it fun. A lot of the people we interviewed shared how looking to improve things makes work more interesting, exciting, and enjoyable—not just for the individual, but for those around him or her as well. Our research revealed that when someone looks for new possibilities for improvement, the odds are 11.8 times higher that the resulting work will inspire a positive reaction—like enthusiasm, optimism, or excitement—among team members, managers, and supervisors.

Now it's time to look for improvements in a rather surprising direction: the past.

Dominique Looks at Trends

We recognize that looking to the past for inspiration goes against some people's notions of forward thinking. As superhero fashion designer Edna Mode says in Pixar's animated classic *The Incredibles*, "I never look back, darling! It distracts from the now."

In an ironic twist, seconds later Edna contradicts her own statement. When Mr. Incredible asks for a costume with a cape, Edna boldly refuses, reciting a long series of superhero deaths caused by capes. "Thunderhead . . . cape snagged on a missile fin! . . . Stratogale, . . . cape caught in a jet turbine! Metaman, express elevator! Dynaguy, snagged on takeoff! Splashdown, sucked into a vortex!" She ends emphatically, "No capes!"

Despite the fact that Edna says it "distracts from the now," in reality, looking back at trends in the past helps her create a safe new suit for Mr. Incredible. OK, it's a cartoon. But nevertheless, this scene demonstrates how past patterns can become a crystal ball that helps us create better work in the future.

If you shop online at Amazon, iTunes, or Netflix, you know that these sites have an uncanny ability to recommend things you might love based on nothing but your past purchases and those of thousands of others. They find new ways to please us by looking back at what we've loved before. They do this by using software commonly known as a recommendation engine.

We too can look into the past to see what has delighted people over time. What has lit them up before? Drawn them in? Made them spread the word to others? What do they really, truly appreciate? Looking back in this way, we ourselves can become recommendation engines of sorts. We can become experts on what people love. Along the way, we may even get a glimpse of the future.

We talked to an award-winning project director at Whirlpool named Pierre Crevier about an intriguing look back by his boss, Dominique.

In 2008, government regulators were cracking down on washing machine companies to make their machines more water- and energy-efficient. Machines that did not meet the new mandates could no longer be sold after 2011. "The top-load washing machines that had been in production at Whirlpool for more than 20 years could no longer be modified to meet the new standards," Pierre told us. "So the heat was on. Typical time frames for developing a brand-new product were three to five years. Now we had only two years to design new products from the ground up."

Meanwhile, the washing machine industry was in the midst of a sort of design revolution. High-end front-load machines from Korean manufacturers like LG and Samsung were gobbling up market share at an alarming rate. Conventional wisdom around Whirlpool saw the new front-load designs dominating the industry well into the future. Top-load washing machines were seen as a dying platform, your grandmother's washing machine.

So Dominique's team was basically given the unglamorous task of designing a more energy-efficient dinosaur. They had an impossible deadline for developing a top-load washing machine from the ground up at a time when the whole world believed that front-load machines were going to be the future. "The front-load project was the 'darling of laundry,'" Pierre said. "Front-load was cool, sexy, high-end. We jokingly called our project (formally known as the Vertical Modulate Washer Project) the Redneck Project or the Git It Done project."

But, with the help of a look at trends and some market research, Dominique began to Ask the Right Question. While looking at what people had loved in the past, Dominique saw that there was something very *good* about the washing machines that your mom and your grandma had. People had grown up with top-load washers. They were familiar. The opening was bigger. They were easier to drop clothes into. They had a larger capacity. As a hunch began to take hold, Dominique asked some customers who had the trendy new front-load machines, "In a few years, when you're back in the market, what do you see yourself buying for your next washing machine?" A surprising majority said, "We'd like to see the top loaders come back." Hmmmm.

Pierre explained, "These people essentially said, 'We really wish somebody would come out with a midpriced top loader that would do just as well as the new front-load machines on energy. Because we really loved our top loaders, but we left them for efficiency.'"

In the end, the team's look back at the glory days of the top-load machine, combined with a lot more looking, learning, and market research, led Dominique to propose a new niche machine to fill a void in the marketplace. Rather than just have the Git It Done team create an energy-efficient platform for Whirlpool's few low-priced models, the project would now include a contemporary-looking, high-efficiency top-load washing machine at a midrange price that the market had historically overlooked ($499–$699). Dominique made a powerful case to his superiors, and soon Whirlpool had transformed a project with very low expectations into a $100 million investment in a new top-load washing machine "Everybody was, like, you're crazy," Pierre said.

Crazy brilliant, as it turns out.

The project required lots of persuasion of company executives, long weekends, teamwork, and an insane amount of what Pierre calls "dragon slaying" to deliver on time. However, the new midpriced top-load machines were revolutionary. Whirlpool sold them as fast as it could make them. And that single machine tipped market share 8 percent in Whirlpool's favor. "Our product went from not even being on the radar screen, not even being in anyone's long-range plan, to the biggest project Whirlpool's done in 25 years," Pierre said. Dominique's team ended up winning the chairman's Spirit of Winning Award. The unheralded Git It Done project became known as the best-run project in Whirlpool history.

Difference made.

No matter how significant (or insignificant) a project may be, a look at trends can shed light on what may be eliminated, what may be possible, or even what may be missing altogether. In social media, today's technology allows us to see what's trending on Twitter, YouTube, and across the web. These mini views of what's been happening in the past few days or hours or even minutes can help us analyze even the most recent past, which is helpful. Because even the most recent look back can become a look ahead.

Jacques Looks to the Future

The final direction in which people See for Themselves gets to the heart of discovering new possibilities and making improvements. In its simplest form, looking to the future is an act of foresight that helps us think about impending changes to understand what someone might love—if we took the right steps to bring it into reality. It's the *Field of Dreams* way of looking that says, "If you build it, they will come."

The Netherlands (Holland) is widely known as the bicycle capital of the Western world. Ask most Americans why and you'll get a fairly predictable answer: "It's flat."

There's no question that the Netherlands (one-fifth of which has been reclaimed from the sea) is a flat country. But with that flatness and a location on the North Sea come something else: wind (hence, the windmills). Ride a bike in Holland, and you'll often find yourself pedaling into a headwind that's as tough as biking up any hill. (That is, unless it's raining or snowing. Then it's worse.)

The real answer to why the Dutch people love their bikes lies not in geography but in a very insightful look to the future that began in 1972.

In the postwar era of the 1950s and 1960s, Dutch officials could see that automobiles were beginning to have a very negative impact on the Dutch lifestyle. By 1970, biking as transportation in the Netherlands had dropped by two-thirds. Parking structures, wider roads, traffic lights, and new highways were popping up everywhere. Cars and roads were taking over a tiny country that was simply not built for them.

In cities across the Netherlands, young government revolutionaries like Jacques Wallage (an alderman for the northern town of Groningen) looked ahead and imagined a different future.

Jacques and other administrators saw in their mind's eye an alternative reality to the car-packed, polluted inner cities that were so clearly on the horizon. They couldn't imagine Holland's quaint, centuries-old city centers being torn down for parking garages. Instead, they saw a way for cars to be accommodated, but kept outside of the historic city centers. They pictured a future on two wheels instead of four.

So they created a new civic platform that combined bike-friendly laws, driver education, investments in mass transportation, marketing, and various road projects. They imagined all kinds of ways to make biking irresistible. Cars were banned from the city centers. The cities invested in bike paths instead of roads. They made bike parking free and car parking expensive. They built bike-only shortcuts and bridges that ensured that biking was faster than driving a car. They taught bike safety early on, to both bikers and drivers. They created traffic-calming laws, separate biking lanes, and more housing in the city center. All in all, Jacques and his colleagues spent tens of millions on biking infrastructure.

They looked to the future and created bicycling heaven.

Today, Jacques (who served as Groningen's mayor from 1998 to 2009) can pedal into town without a helmet and look around at a city center that he first imagined, then helped create. His town, the number one biking city in the number one biking country in Europe, was recently voted Best City Center in the Netherlands. Not a bad result of looking to the future.

• • •

Can you see, in your mind's eye, something that others might love? A new idea? A better process? A needed service? A way to eliminate waste? To add value? To make an improvement? Any of us can, if we try. And seeing a future that's bright with new possibilities propels us forward, gives us purpose, and makes work fun.

It's encouraging to know that a fresh look always leads to new ideas. Always. The mere act of looking causes our mind's eye to start bubbling with possibilities. Our vision may be cloudy at first, but one by one, ideas come into focus. And, with practice, sometimes ideas will come flooding in so fast that we find ourselves drowning in great work possibilities. That's the magic of Seeing for Ourselves.

Perhaps the phrase, "Why didn't I think of that?" should really be, "Why didn't I *look* at that?"

Meet Denise and her team and see the Subaru of Indiana auto plant that delivers less waste to the landfill each week than you do at home by visiting greatwork.com or attending one of our workshops.

QUICK TAKE: HOW TO MASTER THIS SKILL

SEE FOR YOURSELF

Observe everything that affects your work.
- Look at what's being done now.
- Be there in person whenever you can.

Watch what people do.
- See how people experience your work.
- Look at what's working and what's not.
- Imagine what can be improved.

Look at the process.
- See how everything that affects your work is done. What's the flow?
- Understand how the work is conceived, produced, and delivered.

Explore other disciplines.
- Look for answers in nature, sports, the arts, and the sciences.

Examine the details.
- Pay attention to the little things.
- Stand on an assembly line. Visit a customer.
- Look at the data.

Look back.
- Notice patterns and spot trends.
- See what has delighted people in the past.
- Become a recommendation engine.

Look to the future.
- Catch a glimpse of changes that are just around the corner.
- Consider opportunities that future conditions might bring.
- Picture a future that you might help create.

CHAPTER 5

TALK TO YOUR
OUTER CIRCLE

CONVERSATIONS WITH PEOPLE WE DON'T USUALLY TALK TO

LEAD TO IDEAS WE WOULDN'T THINK OF ON OUR OWN.

When you hear the word *mosquito,* what associations immediately come to mind?

Do you think of words like these: *buzz, itch, bite, blood, pest, Deep Woods Off?*

OK. So what if we push the associations out a little bit further? You might possibly think of words like these: *jungle, swamp, net, Amazon, West Nile virus.*

Now let's consider for a moment how our brains function. Our thoughts are the result of associations based on past experiences. In this case, we're talking about things we connect with the word *mosquito.* The associations aren't exactly new concepts. They merely demonstrate our brains' familiar neural pathways at work. In other words, they show us where our brain goes naturally when we think of a particular word or idea. We tend to think in terms of set patterns and known concepts. Familiarity rules.

Consider another topic: the ubiquitous plastic bag. What associations do we make with plastic bags? Shopping? Handles? Rips and tears? Recycling? Someone asking, "Paper or plastic?" Again, what if we push the associations out a little further? We might think of things like these: suffocation, child warnings, sandwiches.

We probably wouldn't think of mosquitoes.

At first glance, plastic bags and mosquitoes seem completely unrelated. Taking each one separately, we have familiar associations for both items. But there's no natural connection between mosquitoes and plastic bags that any of us can think of offhand.

Enter a new conversation.

We talked to Julia after she traveled to Africa with her neonatologist husband, Tim. As they toured Uganda and Kenya, they saw wide African skies; banana and vanilla plantations; rhinos, elephants, and giraffes. But they were also there to learn about infant healthcare and humanitarian issues. As they visited an AIDS clinic and orphanage in Subuiga, Kenya, the orphanage owner took them on a walk around the village. He pointed out the abundance of plastic bags that littered the landscape. You see, in Subuiga, there is no curbside trash pickup, no landfill, and no place for the bags to go. Despite the fact that a few enterprising youngsters collect the bags and fashion them into makeshift soccer balls, the landscape was still littered with them. The orphanage owner suggested that the problem was more than simply aesthetic.

"Every one of those plastic bags will last forever," he pointed out, "and each acts as a trap for stagnant rainwater. This means that those littered bags are a breeding ground for millions upon millions of mosquitoes that carry malaria, one of Kenya's three deadliest diseases."

In a fraction of a second, that conversation created a new connection between plastic bags and malaria in Julia and Tim's minds. In that moment, they learned about a connection that had first been made years earlier by Kenyan environmentalist and Nobel Peace Prize winner Wangari Maathai. The orphanage director told Julia. Julia told us. We told you. And now it will be virtually impossible for any of us to hear the words *plastic bag* without thinking of mosquitoes, Kenya, and malaria.

That's a simple example of the power of conversations as mind-opening, idea-generating tools. The fact is, novel ideas are formed by making new connections. When what we know collides with what someone else knows, a new connection is made. This is a simple concept that is underutilized in the workaday world.

Whenever and wherever people with different backgrounds get together and talk, unexpected ideas suddenly seem to click. That's what makes talking to others an essential skill to have in your bag of difference-making tricks.

THE WE IS WHAT ME IS

The connections we make through conversations mirror, with astounding similarity, the activity of the human brain. Before we go any further into the power of connecting with our outside circles, let's take a quick look at how our brains are wired to connect.

This instant.

This moment.

At any given time, 100 billion brain cells are connecting on your behalf in a complex network of electrochemical conversations. There are trillions upon trillions of connections, neuron to neuron to neuron. Every sight, sound, emotion, thought, behavior, and bodily function is a result of neurons talking to neurons at a speed measured in milliseconds.

One neuron never goes it alone.

It can't. It's not made to. It's made to receive and transmit, receive and transmit, which means that every neuron is creating your experience through synchronized conversations with millions of other neurons in a constant, miraculous flow of information. The more frequently the same groups of neurons communicate with each other, the more synchronized and efficient they become. You may have heard the phrase, "Neurons that fire together, wire together," meaning that when groups of neurons repeatedly communicate, they grow a network of channels and offshoots called *neural pathways*. These pathways become deep-rooted and habitual. The upside is that we get better and better at whatever we put our minds to. The downside is that by their very nature, neural pathways become ruts.

Neural ruts are valuable for making sure that we run, walk, and play by social rules and follow protocols. The deeper the rut, the more second nature an activity becomes. We're wired this way for basic survival. And thank goodness we are, because if our work didn't become second nature to us, we'd need to learn it over and over again day after day. The irony is that habitual ways of thinking can keep us from learning and doing new things. And growth and improvement are all about the capacity to change, something that is vital to the success of any company, team, or individual. The naturalist Charles Darwin said, "It is not the strongest of the species that survives, nor the most intelligent that survives. It is the one that is the most adaptable to change."

One of the greatest discoveries of the twentieth century is the understanding that the brain is not fixed, as had previously been thought. It can change in structure, circuitry, and chemical composition. Areas of the brain can take on new roles and functions, and we are wired to create new connections and thrive. The scientific term for this is *neuroplasticity*—"neuro" for neuron and "plastic" for changeable. Change is the catalyst of life and, likewise, the catalyst for all great work. One hundred billion neurons in your head corroborate that fact.

When Julia and Tim were talking with the orphanage director in Kenya, The words *mosquito* and *plastic bag* were two unrelated ideas in their brains—two unrelated neural pathways, if you will. By explaining the link between *mosquito* and *plastic bag*, the orphanage director sparked a new relation, a new connection. Sociologist Arthur Koestler called this "bisociation," the blending of unrelated pathways of thought into a new pathway of meaning. In layman's terms, the moment our neural pathways for "mosquito" communicated with our neural pathways for "plastic bag," a change happened and something new was generated. Emotionally, it was a deeper understanding. Neuroanatomically, it was a new connection.

Dr. Daniel Siegel, founder of the emerging field of interpersonal neurobiology, calls the flow of information between people "the neurobiology of we." In a 2011 interview with *Parabola* magazine, Dr. Siegel said, "You can take an adult brain in whatever state it's in and change a person's life by creating new pathways." The mind, he continues, is something that is shared between people. "It isn't something you own; we are profoundly interconnected. We need to make maps of *we* because *we* is what *me* is."

In essence, we are conversations—linguistic on the outside and electrochemical on the inside. It's conversations that connect people's ideas to other people's ideas, and it's conversations that connect one person's neural pathways to another's.

What a relief it is to know we don't need to have all the answers ourselves—to know that going it on our own is not only unnecessary but, in fact, unnatural.

INNER- AND OUTER-CIRCLE CONVERSATIONS

According to a study published in *Scientific American*, we each speak an average of 16,000 words per day. While you're being awed by that fact, consider how many people you actually talk to while you're busy chatting away. We like to imagine ourselves conversing with a very rich and diverse variety of people every day. But separate research studies show that we routinely talk to a very small group of the same people over and over again.

Most of us feel that we converse with about a dozen people on a regular basis, and that's true (studies say that the number is somewhere between 7 and 15). But our true inner circle—the group we talk with the most—is even smaller. The fact is, we talk to the same 5 or 10 trusted confidants, allies, and buddies about 80 percent of the time. That means that close to 13,000 of our 16,000 daily words are directed at a very small group of friends and confidants. These closest coworkers, team members, family

Inner- and outer-circle conversations

members, and friends make up our true inner circle. And this is a comfortable place to start having conversations about great work, because these people think like us, care about us, and believe in us. But talking to your inner circle alone can also become a disadvantage—because these people think like us, care about us, and believe in us.

In our conversations with people who do great work, we learned the crystal clear value of talking to people beyond the usual suspects—people in our outer circle.

Our outer circle, in great work terms, simply means those people that we don't normally talk to about our work. That can mean anyone from a friend in another department that we eat lunch with to a total stranger, and everyone in between.

The core principle of connecting with your outside circle is this: grade A objectivity won't come from those who are closest to us. It will come from outsiders. That's where we'll find divergent thinking, unexpected questions, novel ideas, differences of opinion, and added expertise. But, as with other skills, what you bring to the party plays into the equation, too. The people you choose to talk to, the subjects you discuss, the connections you make, and the difference-making ideas that come as a result will all be uniquely yours.

We interviewed a university professor named Barclay who has a special knack for inviting outsiders into conversations about great work. We call it "the Barclay Effect." Over the years, Barclay has developed an uncanny ability to talk to his outer circle while researching two separate doctoral degrees. Barclay admits that the first few times he tried to discuss his work with people he didn't usually discuss work with, he felt a little skittish. "What are people going to think of my ideas? Or of me?," he thought. "Are they too busy or too important to care? Will they think this is something I should be able to figure out for myself?" But Barclay had a useful aha about great work conversations when he realized, "If your conversation is about making a difference, you have license to talk to anyone."

If you remember only one thing about connecting with your outer circle, remember that.

When we engage people in conversations about great work, we're not asking them to solve a problem for us. We're not selling something, nor are we asking for some kind of handout. What we're really doing is inviting them to participate with us in the shared enjoyment of making a difference. It's fun. It's inclusive. It's a good thing. Some folks will play along and lob out an idea or two. Others will jump in with both feet and become partners in our great work journey. Most will participate somewhere in between.

The guiding mantra for connecting, then, is this: it's just a conversation. In that spirit, connecting with others can be stimulating, because we're inviting people to focus their smarts, insights, talents, and interests on some difference we're trying to make. If you're stuck, try these conversation starters on for size:

- "Can I run something past you and get your thoughts?"
- "I'm not quite sure where to start, but I know there's a better way to do this. Can you help me find it?"
- "I have a rough idea for an improvement. Have you had any experience with something like this before?"

And you're in. It's easy. It's natural. Let the conversations begin.

CONNECTING ROB STYLE: CALLING ALL EXPLORERS

Let's return to the great work of Rob, the insurance claims manager from The Hartford. Shortly after hearing about *terra incognita*, or "unknown land," on the radio, Rob gathered a team of claims processors, managers, supervisors, and trainers together to kick-start some inside and outside conversations. He spread out two maps of the United States—one before and one after the Lewis and Clark expedition. He pointed out to his team members how many incredible things were waiting to be discovered out beyond the Mississippi River in 1803. Then he used that as a metaphor for the improvements they needed to make in their own department. He invited his team into the conversation by inviting them along on a journey of discovery.

Rob's training leader, Holly, was first to jump at the chance. She shared Rob's desire to create a better experience for customers, team members, and the company. As the conversation rippled out from Rob's innermost circle to all of the adjusters, supervisors, and leaders on his team, the prospect of going on an improvement expedition snowballed into something that was exciting for everyone. This is not uncommon. Our look at award-winning employees showed that Talking to Our Outer Circle makes us 245 percent more likely to get others excited about our work. Why work in a bubble when there's so much good energy waiting to be tapped if we reach out to others?

When we interviewed Rob, he was notably modest (a common hall-mark among difference makers). As he described that first meeting, Rob said, "I didn't have all the answers. No one person ever does. Lewis and Clark had a whole corps of soldiers, boatmen, hunters, traders, black-smiths, and interpreters. At The Hartford, we had our own equivalent: the varied experience and expertise of everybody on our team. Terra incognita was a way to get us talking—to ask each other, what's out there that we aren't seeing yet?"

In the beginning Rob and his team walked the department, Seeing for Themselves how fellow team members did their work, listening in on calls with customers, reviewing processes and metrics, and studying what high performers were doing in comparison to low performers. As they did so, they began to have a lot of conversations about what worked and what didn't.

Pretty soon, Rob was actively listening to all kinds of ideas from team members: "I gave these guys the big picture and said, 'Help me learn how we can get better at this. Share with me. I want to know what you're seeing, what you're thinking. I can't do this without you. If you see a way to make our customer experience better, come talk to me.' After that," Rob said, "listening made all the difference."

Rob began to hold regular Terra Incognita meetings, face to face and heart to heart. The team members always went to lunch afterward to continue their conversation in a less formal way. It wasn't brainstorming or a troubleshooting exercise, it was a simple discussion, a time to share thoughts and ideas. And it became a favorite meeting for his team. "You can't have conversations in e-mail," Rob said. "You lose the magic. You need the nonverbal cues, the eye-to-eye contact. I'm passionate about that. I believe in interpersonal, face-to-face communication."

Pretty soon the team began to share the thrill of discovery after discovery.

First, Holly figured out that some adjusters were noticeably better at delighting customers than others. Rob and Holly wondered, "What would happen if we focused our work exclusively on those behaviors of adjusters that consistently yield excellence—customer after customer, claim after claim, day after day?" This realization led to a document that Rob and Holly called "Successful Work Behaviors." Originally it was a compilation of 15 best practices for adjusters on the phones. But as the great work expedition forged on, the document morphed into well over 40 behaviors. Then it was trimmed back to 30. It continues to evolve.

The behaviors included things like allowing customers to get their own estimate if desired; making a three-way call among the adjuster, the customer, and an auto shop to expedite repairs; and arranging for a rental car on the spot. What all of the behaviors had in common was that they helped adjusters become more proactive, caring, concerned, helpful, compassionate, and likely to get claims processed quickly, with fewer hassles.

Meanwhile, conversations about improvements were fast becoming the norm for Rob and his team. They found themselves constantly talking to customers, insiders, outsiders, and basically anyone they met about the improvements they were trying to make. Indeed, one influential behavior began as a conversation with a job applicant.

While conducting a job interview, Rob asked a young female applicant, a perfect stranger, to describe best practices that she'd learned at a previous job. She replied, "I always want the customers to know I am there for them through every step. So I tell them, 'I can help you. I can do this.' That gives them confidence, so the call goes better." And just like that, Rob made another connection. He took that thought about confidence back to his team. After a few conversations about delivering more peace of mind to the customer, they altered their standard greeting from a question, "This is Wendy; can I help you?" to a statement "This is Wendy; I can help you." That small change made a big difference in the attitude of each call, giving the claims adjuster a greater sense of responsibility and the customer a greater sense of confidence in the adjuster's ability to make things right.

That one spark from an outside connection helped the team members embrace the importance of adding a more human touch to all their interactions. "We could be dealing with anything from a small fender bender to a serious fatality, from someone who hit a deer on the way to mom's house and walked away without a scratch to someone with serious injuries," Rob said. "Depending on the person and what's going on in his or her life at the time, a conversation can be calm and professional or completely hysterical." After seeing the impact of one small change in their greeting, the team members kept talking about other possibilities, noodling, and refining. Then one day, Ken, a regional VP, suggested that they add the greeting, "Hello, this is Ken. Before we get started, is everyone okay?"

Imagine having just been in an accident and calling your insurance company in that emotional frame of mind, expecting the person you talk with to be all about the insurance claim. Then, instead of asking for your policy number, the person on the other end of the phone says, "Before we start, is everyone okay?" That personal touch changed an ordinary greeting into a human connection, and not just for the customers, but for the claims adjusters as well. Starting with a sincere interest in the customer's well-being, rather than being all about the details of the insurance policy, set into motion a much more mutually respectful conversation, one in which each side trusted the goodwill and good intentions of the other. It was brilliant.

With the Successful Work Behaviors as the adjusters' guide, it wasn't long before unprocessed pending claims dropped from an average of 10,000 to 4,000—a huge difference for any such call center. Customer service surveys also reported record satisfaction across all metrics. Instead of leaving, employees became more loyal. And what had once been a fledgling call center became the number one call center companywide.

So remarkable were these results that company managers from call centers around the country flew in to witness the work firsthand.

Just three and a half years later, Rob was promoted to regional vice president. He now oversees six departments. Today, the same Lewis and Clark map that Rob laid out for his team in Phoenix hangs in his new office in Indianapolis.

CONNECTING BEN STYLE:

THE COMMUNICATION LINES ARE NOW OPEN

There's a whole world of inner- and outer-circle folks we can talk to about great work. But what about the people who are right under our noses? There are people with great ideas whom we pass in the hallway or talk to about everything but our work every day. How can we tear down the invisible walls between individuals and teams and departments and replace them with open conversations? We talked to an accomplished musician from Boston who removed the mystery and made it all look quite doable.

• • •

The conductor of a symphony is given great power over an orchestra (some might even say absolute power). This is due, in part, to conductors' extraordinary gifts, abilities, and training. But it's also a practical matter in order to get 100 or so creative musicians to perform with the same vision and the same feeling—at the same time.

Besides, it's tradition. It's pageantry. It's how classical music has been interpreted and performed for hundreds and hundreds of years. In fact, it's stunning to watch how the all-knowing baton is wielded with such supremacy and honored with such obedience. Each conductor's role is defined by the right to command but not to converse with players. When it comes to contributing great work ideas, violinists and cellists and oboe players are not included in the conversation. In the majority of symphony orchestras, the conductor reigns supreme. End of discussion.

Then there's Benjamin Zander.

While he's respected for founding the Boston Philharmonic, Maestro Zander has a very different perspective—some might even say a rebellious one.

Ben has conducted the Boston Philharmonic Orchestra for more than 30 years. But he's actually been conducting a lot longer than that: nearly half a century. He's a force to be reckoned with at the podium, certainly, but a special kind of force that's not often seen in his line of work. Whereas most conductors are known for their command *over* the musicians, Ben is known for his relationship *with* the musicians. His is one of few orchestras in the world, student, semiprofessional, or professional, where conversations flow both ways, from the podium out and from the players back—all because of an epiphany he had 30 years ago.

"I was 45 years old," he told us. "After conducting for 20 years, I suddenly had a realization: the conductor of an orchestra doesn't make a sound. He depends, for his power, on his ability to make others feel powerful. It was life changing for me. I realized my job was to awaken possibilities in other people."

Initially, there was some question as to how to go about having two-way conversations with players. How could Ben pick the brains of his musicians? How might they interpret a piece? What were their favorite recordings from the past? When would trumpeters most prefer to take a breath? Since communication in a rehearsal is traditionally a one-sided affair from the maestro to the musicians, Ben had to come up with a new way to reverse the flow of ideas.

He calls them white sheets.

Before every rehearsal, Ben places a blank sheet of paper on every musician's music stand. He then invites the players to write down any observations that might help him to help them play the music more beautifully. It is quite simply an invitation to express ideas—not to express a neighbor's ideas, nor to try to guess the conductor's ideas, but to authentically add their own thinking to the music interpretation process.

In the beginning, input tilted toward the safe side. Comments were about practical issues: the agreement between parts, the score, and so forth. But in time, as the players learned to trust Ben's genuine interest, the conversations and ideas blossomed, deepened, and took on a new-found confidence.

The magical thing about Ben's white sheets was the way they lit up participation in each and every player. Soon the musicians were sharing insights and know-how about the music and the experience they were having in every rehearsal. That's really what Maestro Zander was after. In his book *The Art of Possibility*, he says, "An orchestra of a hundred musicians will invariably contain great artists, some with an intimate or specialized knowledge of the work being performed, others with insight about the tempo or structure or relationships within the piece, a subject about which no one has ever asked them to communicate."

The impact of the white sheets on the first few rehearsals was profound. It was career changing—and not just for the players, but for Ben as well. "The white sheets give me insights I could never otherwise gain," he told us. "My power as conductor is not diminished by any means. It is enhanced, as is the power of every musician." That's the impact of connecting with others. This idea leapt off the page in our Forbes Insights Survey, where in 72 difference-making projects out of every 100, employees Talked to Their Outer Circle about their work.

Thirty years later, those blank sheets are in attendance at every rehearsal—and not just at the Boston Philharmonic, but at any orchestra Ben guest conducts around the world. He told us, "After rehearsal, I read every white sheet from every player. If I incorporate an idea from a musician, I make eye contact with that musician the moment the passage is played—I acknowledge him or her during rehearsal and during the performance. Quite magically, that moment becomes *the individual's* moment."

CONNECTING EVEN FARTHER OUT

In 2006, *Wired* magazine coined a new term for connecting with our most distant outer circles. It's called crowdsourcing. Crowdsourcing is about inviting an online community of expert strangers to solve a prob-

lem that a group of employees is stymied by. It's an open challenge. Anyone can play, even a mildly eccentric Canadian electrical engineer whose
lab doubles as a music studio.

Meet Edward Melcarek.

Ed is one of 140,000 freelance "solvers" connected to InnoCentive,
a company that helps organizations solve challenges through crowdsourcing. As an outsider, Ed was able to crack a problem that had baffled
top researchers at Colgate-Palmolive for some time.

The problem: finding a way to get fluoride powder into a tube without
its dispersing into the air.

How could Ed solve a problem rather easily when a team of
chemists at Colgate-Palmolive had not been able to solve it at all? For
starters, he wasn't a chemist. Ed saw the problem from a physics point
of view.

The solution: impart a positive electric charge to the fluoride powder and electrically ground the tube; the positively charged fluoride
particles would be attracted to the inside of the tube. Brilliant. Was the
Colgate-Palmolive team disappointed to be shown up by an amateur?
Hardly. After all, it was their idea to go outside for a solution. And their
idea worked. Ed's neat bit of difference making earned him $25,000 in
prize money—a fraction of what it could have cost Colgate-Palmolive's
R&D staff to arrive at a solution.

Harvard professor Karim Lakhani studies problem-solving effectiveness. In a paper on InnoCentive, he says, "We actually found the odds of
a solver's success increased in fields in which they had no formal expertise. The farther the problem was from their specialized knowledge, the
more likely it was to be solved."

In the case of the chemists at Colgate-Palmolive, they didn't need more inner-circle brainpower, breakthroughs, or funding. They needed a new connection to outside knowledge.

Where do we find outer-circle folks to talk to? That's easy. We start with our inner circle. We can ask friends, family, and coworkers if they know anyone we could talk to about the difference we want to make. Friends of friends is the fast track to outer-circle conversations.

Mark Granovetter, a sociologist at Stanford University, is known for his work in social network theory. In one of his studies, he asked 282 workers—professional, technical, and managerial—how they had found their jobs. Only 16.7 percent had landed their job because of an inner-circle relationship. The remaining 83.3 percent had found them through someone they barely knew. The people who were the most helpful were friends of friends, something that Mark calls the "strength of weak ties"—a pithy descriptive of just how influential outer-circle conversations can be.

The process of connecting with our outer circles is iterative. One conversation leads to another conversation, and so on, as more ideas bubble up, connect, and create pathways to new possibilities. Along the way, we create a community of fellow great workers who will help us refine our improvements into the difference we're determined to make.

EXPERIENCE ALL SEVEN LEVELS OF CONVERSATION GOODNESS

By now it's easy to see how making new connections expands our sense of what's possible. In fact, we've seen seven specific benefits of connecting to look out for:

1. **MORE ORIGINAL IDEAS.** The more fresh ideas we have to work with, the more those ideas interact with one another, knock the rough edges off, connect, disconnect, and reveal possibilities. Even the act of dealing with competing or opposing ideas will help us gain a more rounded perspective overall.

2. **PROXY FOR THE RECIPIENT.** The people we have conversations with are stand-ins for the future recipients of our improvements. If we tune in and listen, others can give us keen insights into the heads and hearts of the people we hope to delight.

3. **NAYSAYING POINTS OF VIEW.** Not everyone is going to understand or like our difference-making ideas. That's valuable feedback that we shouldn't ignore or be offended by. Indifferent, apathetic, even cynical people have a useful knack for bringing fantasy down to earth and calling out challenges, weak spots, and myopia.

4. **SPECIALIZED KNOW-HOW.** Every person we share our improvement journey with will have his or her unique abilities. Maybe one of them has done something similar to what we're thinking about. Or maybe that person has a skill set that we don't.

5. **EXHILARATING CONFIRMATION.** When things are sparking, ideas are connecting, and answers are flowing, there is a parting of the clouds, a sudden clarity of thought, a synchronicity where things suddenly fall into place and make sense. It's euphoric. And it's a sign that we are on to something really cool.

6. **A DIFFERENCE-MAKING COMMUNITY.** Conversations with inner-circle coworkers and friends, plus conversations with outer-

circle experts and allies, can grow into a network of support—a collective intelligence of people whose joint desire to create something great will help make our improvements a reality.

7. **CONFIDENT CLARITY.** Great work conversations establish our trajectory. They sift out the junk, refine our thinking, and clarify our purpose. The true potential of the difference we want to make comes into view.

In the following account, we saw evidence of all seven benefits of Talking to Your Outer Circle in a single story. It's a great example of how a series of conversations helped two people make a dent in one of the greatest problems of our generation.

Imagine for a moment that the poorest people of the world aren't, in fact, charity cases in need of a handout. What if, instead, they are some of the most entrepreneurial people on the planet?

Think about that.

What if the poor, whose very poverty can trigger in us feelings of guilt, pity, and sadness, don't want our charity? What if, instead, they want opportunities to create their own great work? And what if the platform for helping them create those businesses is as simple as a website where regular folks in the developed world can lend money to entrepreneurs in the developing world?

Meet Jessica and Matt.

In 2004, Jessica was a staff member at Stanford Business School and Matt was a computer programmer. Just friends at the time, both of them had visions of making a difference with a cool business idea. But no single idea had grabbed them yet. Then one night Jessica attended a lecture given by Dr. Muhammad Yunus, founder of the Grameen Bank, an institution that provides small loans to poor people without collateral.

"A lightning bolt went off in my head and heart," said Jessica. "Dr. Yunus talked about people in poverty with such respect and dignity. It was a call to action that focused my life's goals."

Just like that, a new connection had been made, an opportunity to make a difference had been sparked, and Jessica thought, "I want to do something similar."

Jessica went back to Matt, and they talked. And talked. And talked some more. They had discussed business ideas many times, but this conversation was different. It was generative, imaginative, enthusiastic, and determined. It caught hold, and it wasn't letting go.

Within about a year's time, their rough-around-the-edges idea had evolved into Kiva.org, the world's first website with the mission of eliminating poverty by connecting people through lending. Note the emphasis on connecting people. On connecting, for example, a nurse in Kansas City with a beekeeper in Ghana, a teacher in Raleigh with a spinach farmer in Cambodia, or a student in Portland with a carpenter in Pakistan, with each connection being made via a small loan—as small as 25 bucks. And that 25 bucks, in time, gets paid back and, if the lender chooses, is loaned to another entrepreneur somewhere else.

Matt says, "Lending is connecting. In a sense, money is a type of information. Lending to someone else creates an ongoing communication between two individuals that is more binding than a donation."

The essence of Kiva's business model is about making a difference, $25 at a time, with as many small business entrepreneurs as a lender wants to connect with. Make a $25 loan, get updates, get paid back, and repeat—all online in a self-regulating lending marketplace, overseen by Kiva.

What follows is by no means an exhaustive timeline but, rather, a snapshot of the conversations that made Kiva a success.

Benefits 1 and 2: More Ideas and Proxy for Recipients

Not long after the lecture by Dr. Yunus, Jessica went to East Africa to look with her own eyes and listen with her own ears. She met and interviewed rural entrepreneurs on behalf of a local nonprofit organization. Her job: to analyze the effect of small business job creation on the health and livelihood of local families. Or said another way, she was having conversations with rural entrepreneurs. Her nights were candlelit explorations, idea-gathering bonanzas, as she put the words and feelings of these entrepreneurs down on paper.

Calls home to Matt were filled with discussions of the unbelievable barriers these entrepreneurs faced. The lack of start-up capital was a common theme.

Matt soon joined Jessica in Africa, following her into Kenya and Tanzania with a camera. Using a set of culturally relevant questions, Jessica and Matt gathered information about the quality of life (or lack thereof) for these people. They learned about small business opportunities for local entrepreneurs and their barriers to growth. The amazing people they talked with through about 150 conversations were an invaluable proxy for Kiva's future customers. Jessica and Matt came home with deeper knowledge of differences that would be loved.

Benefits 3 and 4: Naysayers and Specialists

Another conversation was with the CEO of Unitus, a company working to reduce global poverty. The CEO listened attentively to Jessica and Matt's pitch, then zeroed in on a potential problem. "It sounds like it would be hard to scale," said the CEO. Matt describes this moment as leaving a "pit in my stomach." But it was a critical insight. Lenders would want to know where their money was going, and to whom. The administration of that, plus the potential growth in the number of entrepreneurs and lenders worldwide, could be a scalability nightmare.

Likewise, an astute friend of Matt's pointed out, "You can't just loan money over the Internet." There are, of course, all kinds of government regulations and legal requirements for lending money. A debt is a type of security, and Matt realized that if Kiva was a success, someone in some government somewhere would sit up and take notice. In the United States, that would probably be the U.S. Securities and Exchange Commission (SEC).

Yikes. Was their idea dying right before their eyes?

No, just the opposite.

Their idea was being expanded, challenged, developed, and refined. It was on its way to becoming real. And naysaying points of view were helping them get there.

Jessica immediately went in search of legal support. She knocked on a lot of doors. Most people she contacted were wary of the murky territory of securitization. One day she called 47 lawyers. But the forty-eighth, a lawyer named Kiran Jain at the law firm of Bingham McCutcheon, caught the vision and helped set Kiva up as a nonprofit.

Around the same time, Matt picked up the phone and called the SEC. He cold-called a government behemoth. Who does that? But at the same time, what did he have to lose? The idea was still in its infancy. He just wanted to know how the SEC would react if Kiva launched. Matt says, "This experience helped reinforce a lesson I have applied many times since. Even large, scary organizations are made up of normal people, and there is a lot to gain by simply reaching out to them in a transparent way." Five minutes after calling, Matt was talking to an agent. After a series of conversations, the agent helped Matt and Jessica make a crucial decision: there would be no interest payments as part of the lending—no interest would be returned to users. Without interest payments, the SEC was unlikely to consider the loans to be securities. In describing the instrumental help of the SEC agent, Matt says, "Right away, he identified with the social mission and was incredibly helpful." People with specialized know-how are fairly easy to pull in when they have the opportunity to help make a difference.

Benefit 5: Exhilarating Confirmation

In the spring of 2005, Matt and Jessica decided to beta-test the Kiva website in the spirit of inviting more feedback as well as testing their idea for its potential. Seven small business entrepreneurs in Tororo, Uganda, were listed as potential start-ups seeking funding. Moses Onyango, a friend in Tororo, helped organize the entrepreneurs, while Matt and Jessica put the word out to 300 friends and family via e-mail. All seven entrepreneurs, who needed a total of $3,000 at $25 a lender, were funded in a weekend.

Benefit 6: A Difference-Making Community

Moses, who had helped Matt and Jessica organize the first seven loans in Uganda and an additional 50 after that, started blogging. He chronicled the successes and challenges of the entrepreneurs on the Kiva website.

Then something happened: a groundswell.

Groups of people started making connections to the Kiva idea. A network of channels and offshoots began to grow into a community—a community with the joint desire to help small entrepreneurs.

The *Daily Kos*, one of the world's largest blogs, with a readership of more than a million, wrote about Kiva. That morning, $10,000 in new loans hit the Kiva website. E-mails poured in, many of them from microfinance institutions around the world, including Bulgaria, Rwanda, Nicaragua, and Gaza. These institutions wanted to list their own loan applications on the website. With their cooperation, the scalability issue—the pit that had been in Matt's stomach—could actually be solved. It was a matter of expanding the Kiva concept to a network of partners to increase its visibility and influence.

Then Premal Shah, a total stranger, showed up one day out of the blue. Premal had just returned from a sabbatical in India, where he was working at a microfinance institution. Matt describes Premal as "the missing piece of the puzzle. Jessica and I were confessional, careful, thorough, strategic, and technical. Premal was passionate, charismatic, brilliant, wildly enthusiastic, and reckless." Premal had spent six years at PayPal, alongside coworkers who would go on to found or cofound YouTube, LinkedIn, and Yelp. His specialized knowledge of web-based payment systems and his willingness to take risks were perfect complements to the skills of Jessica and Matt.

Finally, with the support of so many believers, Jessica and Matt were able to select "a group of people who possessed more drive, energy, and pragmatism than money can buy." They gathered a community of friends, coworkers, and allies who were ready to "turn a project into an institution."

Benefit 7: Confident Clarity

Step by improvement-making step, Jessica and Matt's hunch evolved into a nonprofit that, to date, has loaned almost $300 million to more than 700,000 entrepreneurs in more than 60 countries worldwide. Those are the figures as of the writing of this book. They change by the minute.

The nature of Jessica and Matt's work, the pathways they pursued, and the discoveries they made were all informed and inspired by conversations.

Jessica and Matt did not start out as experts in foreign aid, microloans, or international finance, but through conversations, one after another after another, they became the people who could make the difference they dreamed of making.

Can you think of someone out there that you need to talk to about your work? Someone who could shed a little light? Add some expertise? Or challenge your difference-making ideas in a helpful way? Can you ask your friends if they have friends you can talk to? Our look at award-winning work showed that talking to such people makes our work 337 percent more likely to affect bottom-line financial results. Not a bad reason to start Talking to Our Outer Circle.

◎ TALK TO YOUR OUTER CIRCLE

Have conversations with people in your inner and outer circles.
- Pay attention to new thoughts and ideas.

Invite others to join your great work expedition.
- Tap into people's natural desire to share opinions.
- Introduce others to your hunches.
- Ask what they might improve.

Make sure one conversation leads to another.
- Ask people whom you should connect with next.
- Use tools like LinkedIn and Facebook to expand your circle.
- Consider crowdsourcing far beyond people you already know.

Gather all you can from every conversation.
- Seek specialized know-how.
- Explore naysaying points of view.
- Collect original ideas and seek points of clarification.
- Keep a log of all the great ideas you hear.

CHAPTER 6

IMPROVE THE MIX

WE FIND IMPROVEMENTS WORTH MAKING

BY ADDING AND REMOVING IDEAS UNTIL EVERYTHING FITS.

The first three difference-making skills will give us a lot of innovative new ideas to work with. Now what?

People who deliver unexpected value don't just go around improving things willy-nilly every time an idea pops into their heads. They look before they leap. They think before they do. They work in broad strokes before they add the finishing touches. In short, they create changes mentally before they create them for real.

Our look at great work moments revealed that difference makers are good at thinking over, sketching, planning, shaping, and fine-tuning the changes they have in mind. The skill that we call Improve the Mix allows difference makers to consider the potential impact of an idea, make alterations, and discover combinations of new ideas that may or may not work.

This ability is brought to all of us by a rather significant portion of our brains known as the prefrontal cortex. In the words of Harvard psychologist Daniel Gilbert, "We humans have a marvelous adaptation in our brains that lets us actually have experiences in our heads, before we try them out in real life."

In other words, our ability to see the impact of changes before we make them is an important part of being human. Every new discovery, cool tech gadget, medical cure, book, movie, or pasta salad we love is the result of someone first imagining a new way to delight others and *then* bringing that vision into reality.

But sometimes our brain's miraculous prefrontal cortex can use a little help to bring all of our best ideas together.

That's where Improving the Mix comes into play.

• • •

In the 1920s, Walt Disney Studios was an exciting place to be. Film animation was literally in its infancy, with some of the first cartoons—black-and-white features like "Steamboat Willie"—springing to life on the screen. But animation was then, as it is now, a very costly and time-consuming process. Artists had to draw 24 pictures for each second of finished film. For that reason, comic book–like "story sketches" were used to plan sight gags and story elements beforehand. In the early 1930s, a Disney animator named Webb Smith drew some scenes on separate pieces of paper and pinned them up on a bulletin board to tell a story in sequence, creating the first known animation storyboard. Storyboarding allowed animators to imagine the effectiveness of each joke, plus the overall flow and likability of the story, and make changes before a single animation cell was ever drawn. Walt loved the idea, and in 1933, "The Three Little Pigs" became the first Disney animated short to be completely storyboarded before it was produced. Storyboards then began showing up at other animation and live-action studios as well. Later filmmakers from Alfred Hitchcock to the Coen Brothers to Ridley Scott wouldn't dream of shooting an expensive scene without first seeing it worked out as a storyboard. Here are just a few of the many advantages of storyboarding:

1. It is visual.
2. It is flexible and moldable.
3. It identifies problems and organizes solutions.
4. It is interactive and fosters collaboration.
5. It is helpful for generating ideas and making decisions.
6. It saves time and money lost in executing bad ideas.

Of course, storyboarding is rather specific. There are as many different methods for exploring improvements as there are professions. Architects use blueprints. Managers use whiteboards. Process engineers use diagrams. Web developers use wireframes. Industrial designers use CAD software. Brand consultants use mood boards. Football coaches use Xs and Os. There are an infinite number of ways to play with new ideas before we make them real.

One designer we interviewed so desperately wanted her long-awaited kitchen renovation to turn out beautifully that she had her cabinetmaker create and install cardboard replicas of all her cabinets and appliances first. That allowed her to walk around in her new kitchen for a while—to live with it and check the heights, widths, storage options, walking areas, accessibility, and flow before everything was set in stone and tile and steel. Obsessive? Yes. Crazy? Probably. But we visited her kitchen. Not only is it beautiful, but everything seems to be right where it belongs.

The point is not that Improving the Mix needs to be elaborate or difficult; it's that difference makers know how to work loose, to model, fine-tune, and play with ideas before they execute them to find changes that are likely to succeed.

Because so many professions carry their own modeling traditions, we don't suggest that there's any single best way to work with the mix. We can sketch, whiteboard, diagram, prototype, or put ideas on 3 × 5 cards and move them around the conference room table, all with great success. What matters isn't exactly *how* we work with the mix, but *that* we work with the mix. Our Forbes Insights survey of employees and managers showed that Improving the Mix is a factor in 84 percent of all instances of great work.

Twentieth-century design icon Charles Eames, creator of the classic Eames Lounge Chair, said, "Toys are not really as innocent as they look. Toys and games are preludes to serious ideas."

In a sense, models, sketches, and diagrams are toys that give us a way to play around with our work. They let us throw ideas at the wall, like spaghetti, to see what sticks.

When used deliberately to create change, a model allows us to look at the elements of change that are staring us in the face and ask: Will this improvement make a difference? Will people love it? How desirable is it? How cool? How doable? How profitable? How well does it integrate with the good we started out with?

Improving the Mix is where we get to be creative. We're toying with possibilities. And that's an exciting place to be. In the process, we can get deliberate and mindful about the differences we are trying to make. We can mess around with improvements, look for simple alterations that have worthwhile effects, and experience the magical moments when everything seems to fall into place. Difference makers accomplish this with three simple but powerful instruments of change:

1. Add.
2. Remove.
3. Check for fit.

INTRODUCING THE MIX MAP:
ADDING, REMOVING, AND CHECKING FOR FIT

To see difference making in action, we created a simple model for analyzing great work that we call the *mix map*. A mix map lets us put great work under the microscope to see difference making in action, to imagine what was going through the difference maker's mind, and to pick apart what that person did and didn't do to create positive change. What were the iterative steps? Why did one improvement make the cut when another did not? In just a moment, we'll see how mix maps help us understand the good elements that a project started with, what someone did to add value, and how those changes made a difference people loved.

Let's take a look at a variety of mix maps and see how people add, remove, and check for fit to make good projects great.

Simple Addition

Much of the great work we've discussed so far was the result of adding something new to the mix: adding international students to a rural school, a kingfisher shape to a bullet train, or a kinder greeting to an insurance company call center. Examples of simple additions are all around us: suitcases plus wheels; taxis plus credit cards; online maps plus satellite photos; car seats plus seat warmers.

Indeed, the power of adding is so positive and addictive that it's important not to lose sight of our beginning question, "What would people love?" Some people add so eagerly that they wind up adding things that no one cares about. They succeed in making things different *without* making a difference people love. That explains why there are dozens and dozens of features on a DVD player when you use only four.

Someone has added to death.

Indeed, one key to making a difference is to add just what's needed and nothing more. That's the trick. The difference maker's art is to make additions that improve the whole and make it better—not the same or worse. It's not always easy, and it's not always black and white, but the difference-making skills act as guidelines to help us make the right kind of additions to the mix. If we are good at asking, seeing, talking, improving, and delivering the difference made, our chance of making the right additions increases exponentially.

. . .

Not long ago, David was on a fund-raising committee for a local Boy Scout troop. His experience is a simple but instructional example of working with the mix.

For years, the scout troop had held the same breakfast fund-raiser. It was successful. A simplified mix map of the good the committee started out with looked like this:

GOOD MIX

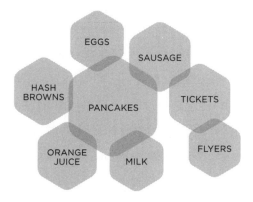

Scout committee's mix

There it is: a simple breakfast fund-raiser. People came, paid money, and ate. The annual breakfast had always managed to net around $1,100. But this year the troop had more boys, more activities, and greater costs to deal with, so the committee members needed to amp up the fund-raiser in some way. They needed to make a difference.

Wisely, though, the committee members didn't brainstorm only around the objective of raising more money. Instead, they wondered, "What could we do that the boys and their parents would love?" In other words, they Asked the Right Question.

You can easily imagine the brainstorming session. Some people thought of adding new menu items: sweet rolls, smoothies, or breakfast burritos. But as they imagined the possible impact of these changes, none of them seemed likely to make a big enough difference. Other ideas included more frequent fund-raisers (quarterly Boy Scout breakfast, anyone?), door-to-door magazine sales, a concert, and a car wash.

This last idea got the juices flowing.

Car washes were low in cost, but high in return. When they first imagined that new combination of elements, it seemed that a car wash might indeed *fit* with a breakfast. The boys could wash the cars while the owners ate their food. They could charge extra money for the car wash. The cars would get clean. But then they might get dirty again as the boys tried to wash nearby cars. Without proper supervision, water fights would ensue. Someone would have to drive the cars into and out of the washing station. The committee members imagined 16-year-olds driving the neighbors' cars. There would be legal liability. Arrgh. Never mind the car wash. It was an okay idea—just not with a breakfast.

When a new addition, like the car wash, isn't dramatically making the mix better, we should feel free to toss it. The elements of a better mix won't clash or fight with one another. When you hit on a brilliant combination, you can feel it. Everything just fits.

Fortunately, the idea of a car wash sparked an unexpected connection in one of the committee members' mind. "Hey," he said, "maybe we can't do a car wash. But I have a few friends with vintage cars and hot rods. What if we added a car show?"

Hmmm. A car *show*. First there was a pause for consideration. Gears were turning. Then the committee lit up. "I know some guys with old cars, too." "I'm friends with a car dealer." "My neighbor has a restored Model T." And on it went.

Simple as it is, the new mix looked like this:

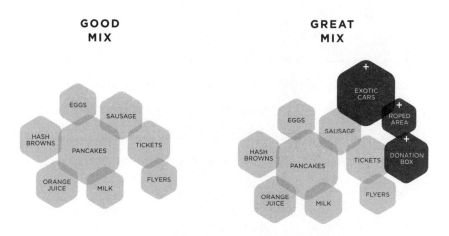

Scout committee's mix

The more the committee members talked about a breakfast and a car show, the better the ideas seemed to fit. "There was a sort of instant compatibility," said one committee member. "Boys and dads and food and cars—it didn't take a genius to see the connection." The committee could immediately see that—as long as their auto-collector friends came through—pulling off a car show would be pretty easy. Get some cars. Create a roped-off area in the parking lot for the show. Create a sort of museum atmosphere. Add a second donation desk at the gate. Voila! A Boy Scout breakfast *and* a car show.

And their intuition was spot on. People loved it.

Looking at the differences that were made, we can see how adding the car show made the fund-raiser better in many ways. Flyers for the event had a catchy new hook. There was curiosity and excitement that hadn't been there before. People who drove by the breakfast could see from the Model Ts and Thunderbirds in the parking lot that something cool was going on. More people came. And those who came spent more money. We discovered in our study of award-winning work that improving the mix makes a project 278 percent more likely to affect an organization's finances. In the end, adding a car show to the breakfast quadrupled the amount of money the scout troop earned that year. The combined event brought in more than $4,000. That'll pay for a lot of Dutch oven dinners, campouts, and pinewood derby cars.

• • •

Just as the fund-raising committee contemplated several other ideas that didn't quite fit before it added a car show, it's not uncommon for difference makers to think of and reject a lot of ideas along the way to a great new mix. Having lots of ideas and combinations to consider in the first place is key. The Italian sociologist Vilfredo Pareto described people who make a difference as being "constantly preoccupied with the possibilities of new combinations." That's a meaningful insight. Difference makers are constantly weighing potential changes and their likely outcomes. They are always curious to find out what happens when they introduce a new element or two to the mix. They are absolutely, without a doubt, preoccupied with new combinations.

Sometimes they do this rather organically (like Jonah and his friends at Little Miss Matched). Sometimes they do it methodically (like the stroller design team at IDEO). But difference makers are ever experimenting with new combinations of value.

Improving by Removing

There's something deliciously counterintuitive about the next instrument of change. Often, when we decide to make something better, our first impulse is to add something new. But difference makers also know the value of removing unwanted, unnecessary, or even irritating elements to make something better. Back in the fifteenth century, Leonardo da Vinci said, "Simplicity is the ultimate sophistication." Whether it's replacing a mass of buttons on an MP3 player with an elegant scroll wheel or reducing the amount of sugar in sweetened cereals (as Lucky Charms and Trix have recently done), removing something can be a great way to make a difference that people love.

Removing can be about eliminating time from a production process, reducing the complexity of a website, removing undesirable features from a product, or any other improvement that involves taking away something that's not loved.

The removing process can begin by looking at the mix you're starting with and wondering whether anything feels wrong. Avis Rent A

Car did this when it took away the check-in line for Preferred cus-tomers, allowing them to walk straight from the plane to their car. Paperless bill pay, no-iron dress shirts, and smartphones without keyboards are all great examples of removing. We already discussed Edwin Land, who removed darkroom processing from photography, and Denise Coogan, who removed trips to the landfill for Subaru of Indiana. Here's a rather brilliant removal from the world of house-hold appliances:

In the late 1970s, a middle-class Englishman named James was frus-trated when his top-of-the-line vacuum kept losing suction. Upon inves-tigation, he soon found that vacuum bags become clogged with tiny particles of dust, causing even the best vacuum cleaners to become less and less efficient over time. He had a hunch: could airflow and suction be maintained by eliminating the bag altogether? Surely the world would love a vacuum cleaner that never loses suction.

What to remove was clear. But the technology that would make it possible was not. The idea stayed with James for a while. "It was in the back of my mind, and I started looking for technology that would solve the problem," James explained. As he continued to noodle on this problem, one day he was at a lumberyard, and he noticed that all the woodworking machines had ductwork that went up onto the roof to a huge cyclone about 30 feet tall. "It works by spinning the dusty air around so that the particles fall to the bottom and the clean air goes out the top," he explained. "I realized [the cyclone] was taking fine dust from these machines all day long and separating it out without losing any suction—I suddenly thought, 'Would this work in a vacuum cleaner?'"

Time to work with that mix.

"So I raced home and made a cardboard model and connected it to my vacuum cleaner. Within about an hour and a half, I was pushing around the world's first vacuum cleaner that doesn't lose suction." James found that he had to add something in order to remove something. His mix looked something like this:

GOOD MIX   **GREAT MIX**

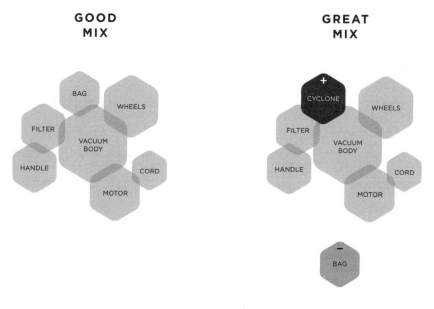

James's mix

Some improvements happen in an instant; others take time and adjustments. James's great mix took more than 5,000 models and prototypes before it was ready to share. After all that effort working with the mix, when James took his idea to vacuum manufacturers, they didn't love what they saw. Almost every major vacuum manufacturer looked at James's great mix as a threat to approximately $500 million in annual vacuum cleaner bag sales.

James would have to go it alone. This would seem to have been a gift now that the Dyson vacuum is a household name. But take all the proto-typing and technology and brilliant research away and Dyson vacuums are a simple story that started with removing the bag.

Checking for Fit:
Chasing Harmony in the Mix

Inspiring as his story is, most of us aren't entrepreneurs like James Dyson. Our job is to take the projects we have and make a difference the way Marty at Motorola did when he removed the car from the car phone. We need to find ideas that keep the good we started with and make it better in ways that everyone around us can buy into, support, and make happen. Our ideas for change need to fit in well, both with the good we started with and with other changes we're making at the time. That's where checking for fit and assessing relationships between ideas really comes into play. While simple improvements to the mix—like adding honey and nuts to Cheerios—are relatively easy to imagine in our heads, some projects involve managing the domino effects of doz-ens of additions and removals all at once. That's where working with the mix really pays off.

Finding harmony in the mix really comes down to a single word: rapport. We're used to hearing that word applied to people or groups, but here we're applying it to the ideas, thoughts, or proposed changes of a project instead.

The most basic rule of checking for fit is that all the elements of our great work project get along together. There's compatibility, harmony, and synergy. Every idea makes the others better.

SWIMMING IN PERFECT HARMONY

The world loves fish. But whether we're talking fish tacos or salmon filets from Costco, fish has to come from somewhere. In the past 50 years, we have been fishing the oceans at an alarming rate. Half of the world's fish stocks are either extinct or nearly extinct. Of the types of fish we love the most—salmon, tuna, halibut—90 percent have collapsed. This has put the world's top chefs in a tough spot. How can they keep serving fish as wild fish stocks continue to decline?

It's obvious that fish farming is destined to be a part of the world's future. But is that a good thing or a bad thing?

It depends.

Fish farms, whether they're cage farms at sea or cement pond farms on land, have a tendency to pollute. The crowded fish have a tendency to get sick. The fish don't taste all that great. And most of all, the process is unsustainable. The average *feed conversion ratio* for tuna is 15:1. In other words, it takes 15 pounds of wild fish to feed the tuna for every pound of farm-raised tuna that reaches the table. Not the *smartest* plan.

Around the world, aquaculture experts are trying to solve these problems. But few have changed the fish farm mix in as inspiring a way as a humble midlevel biologist at the Veta La Palma fishery in southern Spain.

. . .

We visited Veta La Palma and learned that its story began as an ecological disaster. The fishery sits on the Guadalquivir River at the southwestern tip of Spain, not far from where the river empties into the Atlantic. In the twentieth century, Argentineans who owned the land at that time built an intricate canal system there to drain the wetlands for the raising of cattle. This proved to be both economically unwise and environmentally disastrous. The cattle ranch didn't make enough money to stay solvent, and draining the land killed close to 90 percent of the birds in the area. Double failure.

The land's fortunes changed in 1982, when a Spanish company named Hisparroz bought the land and used the same canals that had been used to drain it to reverse the flow. The company reintroduced water to the canals and lowlands and turned Veta La Palma into a working fish farm.

Miguel Medialdea joined Hisparroz as a midlevel biologist hired to help the lead biologist, Narciso. Narciso believed in a "close to nature" way of managing the fish farm that Miguel felt good about. He was encouraged by the fact that Veta La Palma was already being run as an eco-friendly fishery. Soon, the two men's shared assignment was to meet changing market conditions by producing more sea bass faster—in as environmentally friendly a way as possible.

The task was daunting.

Increasing fish production meant taking a more traditional approach to fish farming: increasing the amount of wild fish that had to be caught to feed the fish on the farm, and filling the fish they were farming with antibiotics, vaccines, and supplements to keep them from becoming diseased in more densely packed ponds. It was a sickening prospect for a naturalist and ecologist like Miguel, who had dedicated his life to maintaining balance in nature. "Veta La Palma was a perfect place for a fish farm," Miguel told us. "But I imagined it differently. I saw the world's first truly sustainable fish farm."

Miguel is a down-to-earth guy with a desk, a computer, and a small lab in one of the buildings on the fish farm. But he was imagining an entirely different fish farm mix—one in which nature did the feeding and the disease control. He loved Narciso's close-to-nature management model, but he wanted to take it a major leap further. His new mix involved flooding an additional 7,000 acres with estuary water to give the sea bass more room to live, and introducing shrimp, other fish, and microbial populations that would create natural food chains and clean the water. Miguel wanted to remove artificial feeding and waste management from the mix and add natural systems that could do the same things even better. He understood that for the ecosystem to work, birds, the natural predators of fish, had to be reintroduced to the land.

Narciso was immediately supportive of Miguel's new vision, but Miguel's ideas were radical in their ambition. He imagined Veta La Palma as "a place where people would come and see a big aquatic bird park, like a national park, but what they'd really be looking at is a fish farm." His improvement map would have looked something like this:

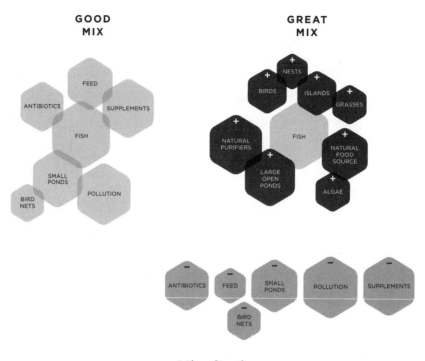

Miguel's mix

If you use a little imagination, it's easy to see why Miguel's ideas proved too radical for the company at first. Build bird's nests to attract predators to a fish farm? Crazy. The board of directors wanted to keep hungry birds as far away from the company's fish as possible.

Use more land to produce fewer fish? Insane. The board was optimistically hoping for just the opposite.

Narciso and Miguel worked hard to persuade the board and others, but for a while only their passion for their improved mix sustained them.

Eventually, Miguel's passion and commitment caused a new CEO to put him in charge of a quality control and environmental management project to gain ISO certification. If you're unfamiliar with ISO, it stands for International Organization for Standardization. Becoming ISO certified helps companies improve their quality, safety, and reliability. While ISO certification is widely sought after, achieving it is often seen as a tedious paperwork project. But Miguel turned that perception on its head. For him, the ISO certification process wasn't a burden. Instead, the assignment gave him authority to change the farm's processes (in the interest of improved efficiency). Miguel could use ISO certification as an opportunity to introduce his new mix—one quality improvement at a time.

As Miguel made quality improvements by filling new ponds, building new islands, and introducing new plants, grasses, phytoplankton, and algae, his mix started to make a difference. Slowly the birds came back, the water became cleaner, and the fish grew bigger. As they did so, Miguel gained confidence in the harmony of his mix.

Others did too.

Early on, Miguel had a hunch that producing larger, cleaner, better-tasting, more sustainable fish could create new market demand among the haute cuisine set. Hopefully, higher prices and increased demand would offset lower production per square mile.

He got that part right.

Our Great Work Study showed that when people improve the mix, their work is 3.17 times more likely to be considered important. Not surprisingly, top chefs like Dan Barber of New York's Blue Hill Restaurant had been looking for a fish like Miguel's—healthy, good tasting, natural, and sustainable. When Dan first tasted Miguel's fish (calling it "sweet and clean, like a bite of the ocean"), he was intrigued. Once he visited the farm in person, he was hooked.

We were equally impressed when we visited Vita La Palma in late 2012. The farm's scale is difficult to put into words. You look out toward the horizon in every direction and see nothing but enormous lakes, marshland, canals, blue sky, and birds. Miguel took us on a tour and showed us that for the most part, the fish are eating exactly what they'd be eating in the wild: plant biomass, phytoplankton, zooplankton, and shrimp. The system is self-renewing. Not only that, but the water that flows from the Guadalquivir River through the farm leaves cleaner than when it went in. It's difficult for nonbiologists to understand the intricate natural processes that convert the river's pollutants like nitrogen and phosphorus into healthy living biomass, but the point is that the farm's ecosystem is so healthy that it even purifies the water. Fish in the farm are swimming in cleaner water than fish upstream.

Veta La Palma fish farm

Dan Barber shares his love of Miguel's fish in an entertaining TED Talk titled, "How I Fell in Love with a Fish." When Dan asks Miguel how he got to know so much about fish, Miguel says, "Fish? I didn't know anything about fish. I'm an expert in relationships."

Nicely put, Miguel.

Even if managing fragile ecosystems isn't in our job description, understanding relationships is key to finding harmony in the mix. If, like Miguel, we become experts in the way things fit together—the way they relate to and benefit one another—we can become masters at working with the mix. Like Veta La Palma, the fish farm that looks more like a national park, our mix can become an elegant and harmonious one.

• • •

We've compiled a short list of clues that suggest we might have landed on a mix with difference-making possibilities. These clues are more like helpful assists than foolproof indicators of success, but they were not arrived at by conjecture. We looked at the experience of thousands of difference makers and hundreds of interviewees and noticed three common indicators that a great mix is coming together:

1. Chain reactions
2. Doability
3. Passion

CHAIN REACTIONS:

THAT IDEA MAKES ME THINK OF ANOTHER—AND ANOTHER

In creative professions like advertising and design, ideas that lead to other ideas are said to have "legs." An idea with no legs stands alone as a one-off—a dead end, a single improvement that begins and ends with itself. An idea with legs, on the other hand, will become a catalyst for other ideas. It'll cause future changes and improvements to fall like dominos. When ideas start to flow, ding, ding, ding, from your mix, you know you're really on to something.

Here's a rather famous example of an improvement with chain reactions that went through the roof.

The name Curt Roberts isn't one that you're likely to know, but Curt told us the details of a rather fascinating difference-making experience.

It happened when Curt was VP of global strategy for Nike. His wasn't your everyday job, but it wasn't all fun and games, either. Curt shared with us how coming into Nike as an outsider, particularly in a leading role, was no walk in the park. "Most people work their way up through the Nike system," he explained. "The culture of the company is so strong that there's almost an organ rejection that happens the more senior you come in."

Earlier in Curt's career, he had worked with McKinsey & Company. Arriving at Nike was like landing on a whole other planet. "I realized right away that this company was run really differently from how management textbooks say a company should be run," Curt said. "My experience at McKinsey said that first, a company sets its strategy around the biggest opportunities for growth. Second, you focus resources on that strategy to create success.

"The way Nike worked was exactly the opposite.

"Support didn't create success; success created support.

"Rather than Nike creating a budget and saying, 'Let's go develop a tennis shoe,' somebody inside the company with a passion for tennis would develop a little hobby on the side. That person would work nights and weekends modeling and prototyping and begging others for help. Then the person would show up with a prototype and a business plan, plop it down on [former CEO] Phil Knight's desk, and say, 'Phil, we need to be in tennis.' And if the idea looked good, Phil's answer would be, 'Okay.' That's how the company grew."

From Curt's perspective, coming in as the buttoned-up alignment expert, that was crazy talk. "As the guy in the top strategy job, it was like, 'Whoa, what are you guys doing?' Why does my job even exist?"

But he learned the ins and outs of the Nike way and embraced the culture. While working with Nike's Techlab—a small Skunk Works team creating projects outside Nike's shoe and apparel business—Curt experimented with prototypes for walkie-talkies, watches, and eventually MP3 players.

"Few people realize that for a very, very, limited time, just a blink really," Curt explained, "Nike had the world's number one market share in MP3 players—that was before Apple introduced the iPod and started eating everyone's lunch."

Meanwhile, a friend on the Nike team named Michael and a few others had a hunch: if runners like to track their progress by keeping logs of their speed, distance, calories burned, and running frequency, wouldn't it be great if their MP3 player could do that for them?

Michael found a viable speed and distance monitor that attached to a shoe, and Nike worked with Phillips to create the Nike/Phillips MP3 Run. The mix map at the time would have looked like this.

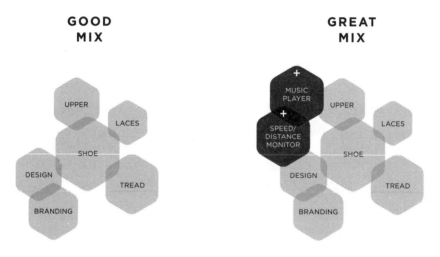

Curt's team mix

"We knew that runners like listening to music while they run, and they love to know how far, how fast, stuff like that," Curt said. "So we really thought our MP3 player and stat monitor was the cat's pajamas. But we weren't getting much market traction. The product was too expensive. The sensor for the shoe was too large. We were working on a smaller, lighter version we could embed in a shoe when we decided to contact Apple. Someone there said, 'Your MP3 Run looks pretty cool. Come talk to us about that.'"

What did the folks at Apple see in the MP3 Run? They certainly saw a combination of elements that was in harmony with a runner's needs. But even more important, they saw future possibilities for connecting with runners in a new way and making running more fun through music—legs, if you will—for what would later become known as Nike+.

As Nike and Apple began to partner on the product, teams from both companies went to work on the future creative implications of that intoxicating new mix.

The team realized that if your iPod could tell you your running stats, it could also be your personal coach. And as long as you were going to hear feedback on your iPod, why hear a computerized voice? Why not hear a sports celebrity like Tiger Woods say, "Congrats, you just ran your fastest 5K ever"?

Curt says, "Once we put the running shoe sensor and the iPod together, it was easy to see we had an insight where one and one equaled three." Apple and Nike's marketing teams soon had hundreds of other ideas based on that original combination of shoe sensor and music player.

For example?

"Let's say you have a great song that really gets you going when you run. Techwise, it was now easy to make it so that when you're starting to drag in your fifth mile, you can hold down the center button and hear your power song. We also realized that with iPod, we would be connecting to iTunes, and iTunes means Internet, where you could share your stats with others. That opened up a ton of possibilities," Curt said. "A friend in Tokyo could challenge you to a contest: 'First one to fifty miles wins.' If you hit five hundred miles, we could give you a free five hundred miler T-shirt. It was just so easy." Nike's overarching goal—to create brand preference by providing a better experience for runners—suddenly had a new friend called Nike+.

The creative domino effects of Nike+, which continue at this writing many years after it was launched, are too extensive to catalog without becoming tedious. The Nike+ team added online record books, rankings by age of runners anywhere in the world, contests (fastest 5k and the like), events (including training that led up to the Chicago marathon where the North side competed against the South side), training programs, weight loss programs, trash talking, calorie counting, and later, with the iPhone, GPS trackers, and running maps.

Did Nike+ make a difference? Oh, yes. In the multibillion-dollar shoe industry, new points of market share are hard to come by. But after the launch of Nike+ in 2006, Nike gained 10 points in market share (worth nine figures in revenue). Why? Curt explained that Nike+ was "sticky" with the running world. Where before, you could easily switch shoe brands when your old shoes wore out, now you had an experience you loved that made you want to come back to Nike again and again.

DOABILITY: RIDING A SUDDEN WAVE OF FEASIBILITY

There are times when those around us just won't get what we're trying to accomplish with a new mix—like the initial resistance Miguel got to his ideas for the fish farm. At those times, it's our own passion, commitment, and sense of doability that tell us that we've landed on a difference worth making. Other times, a new mix comes together that seems so sensible, so doable, that those around us are as lit up by the possibilities as we are. That's a very good sign that we're onto a mix with difference-making possibilities.

When we say that a new mix seems doable, we mean a lot more than mere feasibility. It's not just about finding something that we can accomplish with reasonable effort or within budget. We're not talking about a cost/benefit analysis or resource allocation. What we are really talking about is an overwhelming feeling of attainability—a sudden sense that the change is within reach, workable, and, most important, worthwhile.

When this feeling hits, it's likely to be accompanied by feelings of inevitability, a conviction that we can do this. We must do it. We have the time, the resources, and the talent, and if we don't have them, we know that finding them will be well worth the effort.

Remember the story of Skip Hults, who added international students to his rural school in the Adirondacks? The part of Skip's story that we haven't yet shared is what happened when he took his idea to his faculty and the rest of the town.

No one was expecting Skip to find a solution that would stop the school from shrinking. But when he presented that great new mix, everyone loved it. "I had 100 percent support from the board, the faculty, parents, and the town," he said. "The response was not, 'Let's go form a committee and study this,' it was, 'Yes! Let's make this happen.'"

There was still a lot to learn and a lot to do. Skip and his team quickly realized that they knew very little about the business of attracting international students and catering to their needs. But they would soon figure that all out together. The mix was about to get a little more complicated, but the original idea felt so doable that it gave the team momentum to work out the details of the mix.

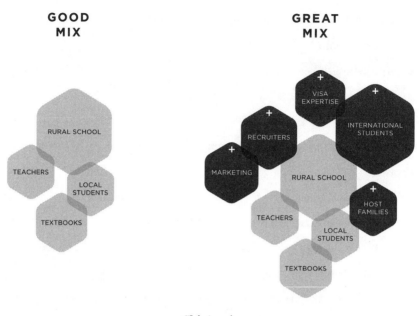

Skip's mix

"People came out of the woodwork to sign up as host families, become experts on student visas, recruit students, and promote the program," Skip explained. "If the idea had been something outrageous and undoable, I don't think people would have come on board so easily. But because it was such a great fit—it clearly met the school's needs culturally, numerically, academically, and socially—everyone just stepped in to make it happen."

PASSION: DOES IT LIGHT YOU UP?

Our research indicated that if passion for a new mix is present, doability and chain reactions are often created in its wake. Think about it:

Miguel's passion helped him turn an ISO certification project into a better fish farm. Curt's team's passion for running with music helped Nike partner with Apple to create Nike+. While we most likely begin any great work journey with a bit of passion, arriving at the right difference-making mix can drive our passion through the roof.

. . .

Adam runs his own gym. Big deal, you might think. If you've seen one gym, you've seen them all. And for 99 percent of the gyms out there, you would be right. The fitness category has been made up of the same good stuff, the same foundational elements, for years: there's the memberships, the workout equipment, music, TVs, locker rooms, amenities, and so forth. But in 2007, Adam had an idea: what if there was a way to harness the energy of exercisers and convert it into electricity? In that instant, Adam's passion for a great new mix began.

At the time, Adam was a personal trainer. He didn't have any experience in electrical engineering, and this was his first entrepreneurial leap. But his desire to make a difference, plus his environmentally conscious sensibility, inspired a can-do attitude. And so he flung himself into it, gym shoes first. His first move was to search "green gyms" on the web to see what was already being done. The results: nothing, expect for a little gym in Hong Kong that was making electricity with elliptical machines. Adam purchased that equipment, but it was substandard for the gym he wanted to create. Back to zero.

Over the next year or so, Adam experimented with various types of gear and gadgetry, jerry-rigged parts from this source and that, read Seth

Godin's book *Purple Cow,* looked into all things green, put out his feelers to connect with like minds worldwde, and, in time, worked his mix into the world's first eco-friendly fitness club: the Green Microgym, head-quartered in Portland, Oregon.

Adam describes what drove him. "I saw this vision of what could be, and I didn't know how I was going to get there, but I just wanted to go for it. I wanted to make a difference, to give people one more good reason to work out, and to do what I could for the planet."

Adam kept many elements from the good gym mix he started with. His gym still has memberships, workout equipment, music, TVs, and locker rooms. But here's how Adam worked to shape that good mix into a great mix: he added elliptical machines and stationary bikes that produce electricity for the building, treadmills that use 30 percent less electricity, exterior solar panels, eco-friendly building materials, non-VOC (volatile organic compounds) cleaning supplies, and recycled paper products. He also scrapped a few things from the good mix: no towel service, no bottled water sales, and no vending machines that refrigerate.

That's the thing about discovering a mix that lights you up. Once that spark is lit, you have the passion to keep right on working: to keep the stuff that fits, toss the stuff that doesn't, and add new stuff that trans-forms good into great.

In 2010, Adam conducted a study that he calls "Our Green Advantage." According to the report, compared to other boutique gyms of similar size, the Green Microgym is making a big difference to the environment every day. By combining human power with solar power, the gym is able to generate 35 percent of its own electricity. That's a 60 percent reduc-

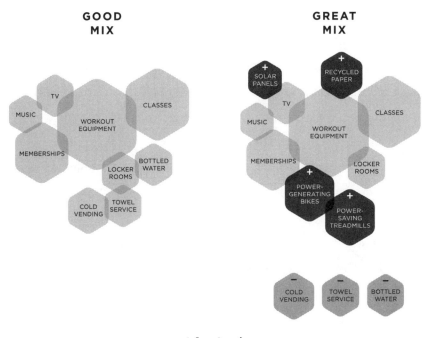

Adam's mix

tion in carbon emissions, or 74,000 pounds—an impact equivalent to 15 acres of planted trees or 81,400 miles not driven by cars.

It's important to note that every individual change that Adam made counts as an improvement to the original good that he started with. Even Adam couldn't (and didn't) manage all those changes at once. He added the power-generating elliptical machine (an improvement that people loved), and later the solar panels (another improvement). He worked with and changed the gym mix one or two elements at a time until he got to the composite great mix we chose to illustrate. But was that the end of Adam's great work journey? No. He's out there making new improvements to his gym as we speak.

IT ALL COMES DOWN TO THIS

Anyone can practice working loose: sketching, diagramming, modeling, shaping, fine-tuning, and tweaking for the better. With practice, we get better at adding and removing ideas until everything just fits.

When you first read the Newcomb School story, could you tell at some point early on that the town would love adding international students to save the school? Could you see that it was a great fit? Could you feel the potential ripple effects before they happened? When you read about Miguel's fish farm, was there a moment when you began to root for the idea, to pull for it, to genuinely wish for its success?

That's the feeling of a great mix coming together. It's a feeling that's available to all of us when we add, remove, and check for fit to improve the mix.

When that feeling comes along, there's only one thing left to do: put our great work out there and deliver the difference.

Watch Dan Barber's fabulous TED talk about Spain's Veta La Palma fish farm at greatwork.com.

IMPROVE THE MIX

Work with ideas to find improvements that are worth making.
- Lay out all the ideas you gathered with the first three skills.
- Play with new combinations.
- Use 3 × 5 cards, sketches, or diagrams.

Add something new.
- Go for volume. Start with lots of ideas and edit.
- Consider how changes affect the good you started with.
- Notice intended and unintended consequences.

Remove.
- Improve by taking something away.
- Look at things that people don't like.
- Imagine ways to reduce and simplify.

Check for fit.
- Don't blow things up.
- Keep in mind the good you started with.
- Look for exciting rapport between ideas.

Watch for signs of a great mix coming together.
- Go for chain reactions. Great ideas lead to great ideas.
- Go for doability. Great ideas feel sensible, feasible, and irresistible.
- Go for passion. If it lights you up, it may light others up as well.

CHAPTER 7

DELIVER THE DIFFERENCE

GREAT WORKERS ARE OBSESSED WITH POSITIVE OUTCOMES.

THEIR WORK ISN'T OVER UNTIL PEOPLE LOVE THE RESULT.

Delivering the Difference plays an important role in every great work story. That's why it's been present in every example we've discussed, regardless of the skill that was highlighted.

At first, it took some sleuthing to understand what was going on in our great work research. Why were there so many comments about award winners "toughing it out," "soldiering on," "not giving up," "staying with it until the end," and so forth? When those references first popped up, we thought, "Hmm—finishing the work sounds important, but also rather obvious. Don't we always need to finish what we start? What makes that insightful? How does getting the job done relate to great work opposed to merely good work? " Is "finishing strong" really a difference-making skill?

Whether in work or in life, we all know the feeling of being in the home stretch. Most of us have gritted it out in a sprint to the finish line after what might have been a months-long marathon of effort. This is the final stage of the hero's journey, where true grit, tenacity, and willpower transform good into great. It's easy to look back on such home stretches with a warm fondness and a memory of achievement. But when we're in the moment, these late-night pushes and last-minute sprints can be scary. They're the crunch time, when unexpected problems pop up and stuff we thought would be amazing turns out to be not so spectacular. It's in these eleventh hours, final battles, and darkest hours before dawn that our true commitment to great work gets tested. All of the skills we relied on to make a difference in the first place are often revisited and compressed as we work at lightning speed to solve problems, to work and rework the mix in real time, and to deliver something wonderful.

One by one, our interviewees taught us that people who do great work have a different set of criteria for declaring a job complete: whereas the typical definition of *complete* is "the work is done," the great work definition of *complete* is "a difference is made."

Think about that for a second.

How much would it change our work if we didn't consider a job complete until we saw evidence that a difference had been made? If we kept on working tenaciously up to and beyond the moment of delivery to ensure that our recipients were truly delighted? Our great work study proved that difference makers not only stay engaged until a difference is made, but follow the results of their work *after* the majority of the work has been done. They insist on knowing what worked and why. They stay with their work just a little longer to follow up, gather insights, gain sensitivity and understanding, and make connections between changes in the mix and differences that were loved. This sort of follow-through then primes them to become repeat difference makers—the kind of people who do great work again and again. Indeed, Delivering the Difference becomes a sort of launchpad for other great work endeavors.

In our Forbes Insights survey, the presence of Delivering the Difference showed up loud and clear. In an astounding 9 out of 10 instances of award-winning work, employees stayed engaged and involved until a difference was made.

That's a skill worth talking about.

Bill Klem was the father of baseball umpires: colorful, judicious, and dignified. He was beyond passionate about America's favorite pastime, declaring, "To me, baseball is not a game, but a religion." The first umpire to use arm signals while working behind home plate, Bill umped for 37 years, including 18 World Series. He became known as "the Old Arbitrator," a deferential nod to his keen eye for calling balls and strikes. On one such occasion, as he crouched and readied behind the plate, the pitcher threw the ball, the batter didn't swing, and, for just an instant, Bill said nothing. The batter turned and snorted, "Okay, so what was it, a ball or a strike?" To which Bill responded, "Sonny, it ain't nothing 'till I call it."

Now, we can't possibly know the true spirit of Bill's reply: whether it was dictatorial or philosophical. Maybe he was just putting a snarky young batter in his place. Or maybe he actually believed that a ball or strike was nothing until he labeled it into being. It doesn't matter. It's the words "'till I call it" that carry something profoundly truthful. Those four little words capture how indispensable postcompletion input can be. Until Bill called the pitch as either a ball or a strike, the batter was alone in a vacuum. It was impossible for him to know whether letting the pitch fly by had been a good decision or not.

Bill was a philosopher, whether he meant to be or not. He reminds us that great work cannot happen in solitude. It's impossible. If the aim is to make a difference for others, learning whether a difference was made and understanding exactly how that difference was made is the final stage of any great work journey.

The fact is, people who routinely do great work develop a heightened sensitivity to whether or not their output is appreciated by others. They demand to know whether the work was noticed, ignored, valued, loved, or hated, and why. They have a heightened sensitivity to delight or disappointment. They can tell if recipients are just being polite or if they really love the difference that was made. They know that their improvement ain't nothing until the recipient calls it.

• • •

In late 2011, we met with a group of designers who create websites for top corporations. These gifted men and women are the makers, the creators, the frontline producers of their company's product. But other individuals—sales reps, customer service reps, and middle managers—handle all the customer interactions. At the time we met, the process for the designers was: get an assignment, do the work, toss the completed job over the wall to someone else, and wonder what happened.

It was no surprise that the work suffered.

When a decision was made to improve work quality, one significant addition to the mix was allowing design teams to personally present their work at client meetings. When travel or budgetary constraints prevented that from happening, the designers requested detailed recaps and reports of what went on at the presentations. This was more than merely a thumbs-up or thumbs-down from the client; they wanted a true accounting of what was said, the smiles and the frowns, the body language, the energy in the room. It was about understanding, learning, and being in tune with what was wanted. Once the designers had a better idea of the difference that had been made or not made, their output improved dramatically.

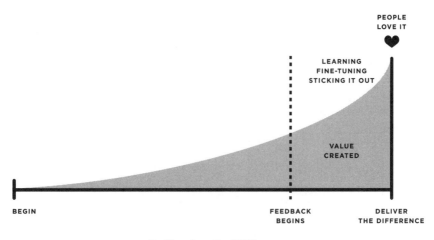

Delivering the Difference

Difference makers don't approach their great work projects casually. From the point when they decide to deliver something new and unexpected, they care about the end point. They follow through until they Deliver a Difference, and they follow up on the difference they deliver. They learn what worked and what didn't. And they carry those findings with them on their next great work journey.

TINA'S PHOTO FINISH:

INSISTING ON A DIFFERENCE MADE

Tina is a professional photographer. But her work doesn't grace the covers of magazines, hang in art galleries, or appear in retail catalogs. Her work is of a far less prestigious, but perhaps more important, kind. She takes thousands of school photographs for preschool through twelfth-grade children each year. While not always known for their excellence, school photographs are the ones we all keep. They become family treasures. They are displayed in hallways, living rooms, offices, wallets, and family albums for generations.

But how can school yearbook photographers Deliver a Difference when they have only a few quick moments to photograph each child?

Imagine the reality of Tina's job. Hundreds of kids are lined up—rowdy, fidgety, and self-conscious. She has just a moment to snap each pupil's photo once or twice and see if she can capture something good, and then it's on to the next kid. It could easily take on the feel of an assembly line—get 'em in, get 'em out, make sure each kid's eyes were open in at least one shot, and do it all again the next day.

But Tina is so determined to capture each child's one-of-a-kind personality that even in the mediocre land of school portrait photography, she captures great shots with astounding frequency.

We talked to Tina about one shot in particular that was taken at a school for autistic students.

Tina began the day with plenty of excuses not to Deliver a Difference, but she chose to ignore them. "Taking pictures of kids is hard enough in a regular setting," Tina explained. "But no other photographers wanted to even touch this school. The young adults there have a hard time controlling their bodies, their behaviors, everything."

The day of the shoot was every bit as challenging as Tina had expected. In the middle of the session, exhausted, she took a deep breath while one more group of autistic students filed into the room. She noticed a twenty-something young man standing in the doorway. He never lined up to get his picture taken. When the session ended, Tina inquired about him. "Josh didn't bring in his form today," the school secretary explained. "His mother will be here soon."

Tina, who technically could have been done for the day, suggested that she have a try at capturing Josh's picture, form or no form. The secretary shrugged her shoulders.

"Okay."

Tina introduced herself to Josh and positioned him in front of the lens. She chose a light gray background to complement his red T-shirt and began to coach him through some shots. None of the images were usable. In most of them, Josh's head swayed into and out of the frame. In some he was drooling. He could rarely hold his gaze forward long enough for the camera to make a connection. It would have been perfectly acceptable for any school photographer to stop right there and call it good. But Tina wasn't focused on being done. She was focused on Delivering a Difference.

She kept shooting. And shooting. There were no more kids in line, so she treated taking Josh's picture like a mini private portrait session: one more shot, then another.

Finally she said, "I got it."

Moments later, Josh's mother rushed in. "I forgot to send these forms today. Am I too late?" Tina introduced herself and explained that she had just finished taking pictures of Josh. Then, hoping to delight, she invited Josh's mother to review them. One by one Tina toggled through the imperfect shots as Josh's mother offered a polite half smile. Then Tina came to the one—the single picture where Josh's head paused and his gaze was fixed directly into the lens. It was only a split second, but Tina had captured it. Josh looked like the kid next door.

Josh's mother began to cry. "I have never been able to get a picture of my son that showed him the way I see him," she said. "Every year we hang his school picture up in the hallway next to my other children's photos, and every year it's a bad picture. But it's his, so it needs to be there. You have no idea what you have done for us today."

In that one moment, Tina saw her work through to completion and Delivered a Difference. Absolutely. Beautifully. And her approach continues to do so. Schools in her area are so in love with Tina's personal touch in photographing children— and the great photos that come as a result—that they commonly request her by name.

KEVIN AND MIKE ADAPT TO MAKING THE WRONG DIFFERENCE

As inspiring as it is to see someone deliver a difference the way Tina did, it's also interesting to see how some people do great work even when their best-laid plans for making a difference go awry. It's hopeful and helpful to know that we can learn to succeed even when the difference we've made is not the difference we intended to make.

When people don't love our work, when our work stumbles, stalls, or otherwise flops, we need to remember that this is just an opportunity to become a more intelligent difference maker. We need to relax into the experience and allow ourselves to soak up some knowledge.

Dr. Carol Dweck refers to this healthy approach to failure as having a growth mindset. Dr. Dweck is a professor of social psychology at

Stanford University. For decades, she's been studying the growth mindset and its counterpart, the fixed mindset.

Her research indicates that those with a fixed mindset believe their success is due to their innate ability and intelligence. A fixed mindset causes people to fear failure; they don't want to try anything that might damage their current sense of ability and intelligence. Their self-worth and identity are wrapped up in not making a mistake, so they gravitate to fail-safe activities that confirm their current status and capabilities.

People with growth mindsets, on the other hand, seek out challenges and activities that expand their abilities. Because they believe that skill and intelligence are developed through effort, they view setbacks and failures as opportunities for growth. "When confronted with a task, people with a fixed mindset ask, 'Am I going to be good at it immediately?' People with a growth mindset ask, 'Well, can I learn to do it?'" The fixed mindset seeks sameness and validation; the growth mindset seeks learning and adaptation.

● ● ●

Entrepreneur Kevin Systrom says, "If I could give any advice, it would be: put it out there, find the people who are vocal about what you're doing, put it in their hands and listen to them, listen to what they are excited about." We were impressed by the growth mindset of Kevin and his cofounding partner, Mike Krieger.

Kevin and Mike created an app called Burbn that helped users share their location with friends and family wherever they were: at a club, a restaurant, a travel attraction, a coffee shop, and so on. Burbn let users keep track of where those in their inner circle of friends were at any time so that they could hook up and hang out. As part of sharing one's whereabouts, Burbn gave users the ability to take a photo at their location and post it online. The exciting new combination of value that they expected to click with customers was location check-ins and live posts plus photo sharing. Kevin prototyped Burbn and sent it to 80 or so friends and colleagues, who rippled it out to their friends and colleagues, so that he might experience the difference it made.

What happened next was a direct challenge to Kevin and Mike's growth mindset.

It turned out that people didn't use Burbn all that much. They really didn't care about checking in and sharing their locations. Plus they found the app too complex and encumbered with too many features. Also, they thought it was too slow.

In short: no love.

But.

There was a glimmer of possibility: users were unexpectedly drawn to Burbn's photo-sharing feature. They weren't using Burbn for any of its intended uses, but they were using it to shoot and share latte photos, dog photos, nature photos, hobby photos, and mundane everyday out-and-about photos.

Someone with a fixed mindset would have clung to the original idea. After all, lots and lots of hours had gone into making it work, and that was the idea that needed to prove successful for the developer's self-esteem and ego to be validated. A person with a fixed mindset would have stuck with the Burbn concept, streamlining its features and increasing its speed. Such a person would have literally fixated on iterating the next version, rather than looking at Burbn as something that hadn't made a difference and was therefore expendable.

Kevin and Mike, on the other hand, looked "no love" straight in the eye and asked themselves: "What was the one thing about Burbn that made a difference?" To their surprise, it was photo sharing, loud and clear. So the two men dove headfirst into understanding every app then available in the photography category.

Consider Kevin and Mike's unique response to not delivering a difference. They wasted no time wringing their hands over their lost idea. Instead, their reaction was, "What did we just learn?" and then, bam, they got right back on the great work horse.

What happened next was a complete overhaul of the first attempted mix. Burbn was stripped of any features that were not related to photo sharing. Then Kevin and Mike set out to solve three problems that no other photography app had yet solved. First, people couldn't take beautiful photos with their phones at that time. Second, it was cumbersome to post a photo to multiple social networks. Third, uploading was a slog.

The answer to the first: cool filters and borders that beautified any photo, added an artsy touch, and made a personal statement about the user.

The answer to the second: instantaneous sharing on all the social platforms, including Facebook, Twitter, Flickr, Tumblr, Foursquare, and Posterous.

The answer to the third: lose the massive file size by optimizing the app for the iPhone's highest resolution, then upload the photo instantly, before tagging activity is even started.

Kevin and Mike's new app let users capture a life moment in a photo, customize its look, write a caption, and post it on their favorite social networks, all with a few clicks. It became obvious that Burbn, as a name, no longer fit, so Kevin and Mike considered the essence of the app they had created. It was an app for posting visual telegrams. Plus, they had designed it to frame every photo in a white square border—their homage to the old Kodak Instamatic and Polaroid cameras. The name Instagram pretty much chose itself.

Kevin has said that Burbn helped them find out "how people were *actually* using the product, as opposed to how they were *meant* to be using it"—a distinction that sums up in a nutshell the beauty of being sensitive to differences made.

In October 2010, Instagram was launched to the iPhone world. It went from a handful of friends as users to the number one free photography app in a matter of hours. In just three months, 1 million iPhone users had downloaded Instagram. When the Android version hit, it took only 12 hours to attract 1 million downloads. As of the writing of this book, Instagram's global community is approaching 50 million users, one of the fastest-growing services of all time. In reality, Instagram is regarded as the first truly international social network, because people worldwide can now communicate across language barriers via the language of photography. In April 2012, Facebook acquired Instagram for $1 billion in cash and stock. That's a good, albeit extreme, example of something we saw often in our research: staying with your work until your output is loved makes you twice as likely to make a difference that can be counted at the bank.

MIKE'S TEAM LEARNS FROM

EVERY LITTLE DIFFERENCE MADE

Sometimes we Deliver a Difference we're proud of. People love it. It's great. It has no drawbacks. But achieving that one difference makes it clear that an even greater difference is possible. In that case, we've done something worth celebrating. We've delivered for sure. But now our bar has been raised. A new goal is on the horizon. Even though we've achieved great work, we need to start over to deliver the maximum difference possible.

O.C. Tanner, the recognition company whose database of great work moments inspired this book, manufactures, among other things, symbolic pins for corporate recognition. Companies use these pins to celebrate employees—sometimes for career accomplishments and sometimes for great work along the way. Highly skilled jewelers handcraft about 6,000 emblems every day, or 1.5 million a year. As you can imagine, the company is obsessed with process improvement.

A couple of years ago, the need arose to focus on a specific step in the manufacturing process: welding. A new electrobonding welding machine was performing below expectations: 36 percent of all welds were bad. Totally unusable. That was an unacceptable waste of time, materials, and money. A team of researchers, welders, process owners, and statisticians decided to do some great work and improve the machine's rate of success.

The electrobonding machine is used to weld a short pin to the back of each emblem. The result is supposed to be a wearable piece of jewelry.

But at project launch, good welds were happening only 64 percent of the time. Mike and his team had a target success rate of 98 percent.

The first step was to reach out to the manufacturer of the welding machine for assistance. But the manufacturer responded with a glib, "That's as good as any of our customers are getting. It's the best machine on the market. What's your problem?" Mike describes that reply as a turning point. "It was up to us."

The team dove in, asking, seeing, talking, and improving the mix. At some point early on, the statistical team got curious about the wet sander. It was used to sand the backs of the emblems just before the weld. Maybe the emblems were too wet and needed to dry first. In prototype mode, the team members tried that idea and found, to their shock, that it was just the opposite: an emblem with a little water on its back actually welded *better*. They had their first clue to a better mix. Before every weld, the welder dabbed a small paintbrush into a vial of water and coated the back of the emblem. Everything else in the process stayed the same. Remarkably, the addition of cheap paintbrushes and tap water boosted the rate of successful welds to 80 percent, a 16 percent point jump.

The team loved it. Everyone was pleased to have Delivered a Difference. But they were far from satisfied. If anything, the success of that improvement generated all kinds of questions about other simple ways to make measurable differences. The team continued to live inside the difference-making process, to participate in it and listen closely for newfound insights and learning.

In time, one team member noticed that if the water on the back of the emblem beaded, the weld was less likely to take. The team experimented with taking an extra half-minute to spread the water evenly on the back of each emblem, and sure enough, the insight was correct. Successful welds continued to rise with that addition to the mix, as did the team's curiosity about what other improvements were possible.

Then a welder came in one day having seen a TV commercial for Joy dishwashing liquid the night before. The commercial touted Joy's ability to reduce beading by spreading water all over a newly cleaned glass. An ingredient that causes this is called a surfactant, a substance that reduces surface tension so that water droplets spread across the surface area. The team added Joy to the water. And that great new mix yielded another boost in the successful weld rate.

Note the value of being tuned in to what each new addition to the mix can teach us, whether it's making a difference or not. For the welding team, every new great mix created a new result, and the input from that result informed yet another great mix. Notice how close the team members stayed to the foundational elements of good throughout. For example, when they realized that water was making a difference, they kept working with water. Each new mix inspired the next—water, plus distribution by hand, plus Joy dishwashing liquid. Together, these three improvements increased the rate of successful welds to 90 percent. That's a 27 percentage point increase in welding efficiency from a few dabs of soapy water. Mike, the team leader, says, "Most improvements are not grandiose or showstopping. They are small, incremental changes that add up to a bigger solution. That's where great work comes from."

The rate of successful welds hovered around 90 percent for quite a while. But the team was on a mission. Its members kept observing every detail of the welding process, absorbing input and looking for insights. It occurred to them one day that they had not considered automation. Were there any steps where automated technology could replace the human hand? That sparked all kinds of new additions to the mix. Eventually, the application of soapy water by hand was replaced by application with a hypodermic needle. It was more precise and efficient. That addition created a new great mix that tipped the successful weld rate a few percentage points closer to the team's goal.

Next, a team member decided to look at the issue of pressure. When the welder held down the emblem by hand, was there an ideal pressure that improved the chances of a successful weld? The answer was yes. The team discovered that the ideal pressure was between 40 and 45 pounds. But no human hand has the stamina to apply 40 pounds of pressure 600 times a day, so the team created a pneumatic air clamp that held down the emblem at the moment of the weld. This was the fifth and final addition to the process and the final great mix.

Today the successful weld rate is well over 99 percent. It took lots of asking, seeing, talking, improving the mix, and delivering differences. But each improvement was like a shot of great work adrenaline. As the team members experienced the difference made again and again, they became better than they were before. That's why the team leader, Mike, is less impressed by the way the process changed the machine than by the way it changed his team. "It's all about becoming sensitive to improvements that actually make a difference," he says. "At some point that welding machine will become dated and die out. But the insights we gained will carry us forward to our next opportunity."

YOUR GREAT MIX CAN INSPIRE OTHERS

It's amazing to think that every difference we deliver acts as a spring-board to other differences, whether we make them or someone else continues the cycle for us. The fact that our great work keeps multiplying means that we're each in a position to play a small but important role in the vast evolution of products, services, or ideas that make the world a more safe, fun, comfortable, beautiful, interesting, healthy, or joyful place to live.

In *Great Work*, we've seen that the person who receives our work can be anyone. At work, it may be a customer, a manager, or a peer. In life, it may be a family member, a neighbor, or a friend. But having someone to Deliver a Difference for is important, because if even one or two people are delighted by our difference, there can be ripple effects that go further than we might think.

On Christmas Day 1965, Sherm's ten- and five-year-old daughters, Wendy and Laurie, were bouncing off the walls with Christmas joy. His wife, Nancy, was pregnant and had just learned that the baby would have to be delivered on December 28 because of Rh-factor problems. Looking at the nerve-racking effect his energetic daughters were having on his anxious wife, Sherm knew that he had to get the girls out of the house.

It had snowed 10 to 12 inches on Christmas Eve. The dunes behind their home in Muskegon, Michigan, beckoned. They tried sledding, but the sled rails were cutting through the fresh snow and hitting sand, so the sled wouldn't glide. Sherm needed to come up with a difference that his girls would love. He and his daughters tried standing up on one of

Wendy's Kmart skis to ride it like a skateboard. It was surprisingly fun, but the single ski was too thin. So Sherm went to the garage, found a few scraps of quarter-round floor molding, and screwed both of Wendy's skis together.

At first Wendy was horrified (the skis were her pride and joy). But as soon as she began to ride the new contraption standing up, she was delighted. While looking for a simple way to entertain his daughters (and give Nancy some peace and quiet), Sherm had discovered a way to mix snow and surfing and Delivered a Difference. The girls loved it.

Sherm told us about that day. "Those kids were having an absolute ball," he said. "They were fighting over who would get to ride it next. The neighbors went nuts and played on it all day long. Later that afternoon, my wife yelled out the door that we should call our new stand-up sled the 'Snurfer,' for 'snow' and 'surfer.'"

It was Christmas week and Sherm had time off, so the next day he went out to every Goodwill store in the area to buy up all their old water skis. Soon Sherm's dad, who lived a block away, came over and gave Snurfing a try. He was a big man—6'5" tall—and after riding a few feet, he fell off, sending his board careening down the hill. "It was my dad who gave us the idea of putting a little rope on the front," Sherm explained. "The original intent was just to keep the board from sliding away. But we found out the tether helped with turning and braking as well."

At the insistence of daughter Wendy, who felt that the toy was too much fun not to share, Sherm connected with the Brunswick Company (which had a bowling and billiard factory nearby) and found a buyer for his new toy. Brunswick's attempt to enter the toy market with the Snurfer became a Harvard case study in how *not* to market a product. But in spite of those blunders, over the next several years close to 800,000 Snurfers were sold.

Sherm, who admits he never saw the Snurfer as anything more than a replacement for the sled, said, "Some friends and I used to go out on the dunes and ride these crazy things I had made. We had such a ball. I remember sitting there one sunny afternoon and saying in jest, "You know, this is too much fun. It's gonna be in the Olympics someday."

From 1965 to 1979, Sherm and the local community college sponsored Snurfing contests on the dunes in Muskegon. "College kids picked it up just like the hula hoop," Sherm said. "The competitions got bigger and bigger. We had so many divisions that we ended up moving to a small ski area called Pando near Grand Rapids.

Sherm's Snurfing competitions were the early beginnings of a snow-surfing culture.

In garages from coast to coast, fanatics began to tinker and modify their Snurfers, working with the mix to add bindings and other improvements. At the 1979 Snurfing championship in Grand Rapids, a young Snurfer from Vermont showed up with a board of his own making. His modifications disqualified him from the regular Snurfing competition, but rather than sending him packing back to Vermont, the judges created a new division just for him. As the only racer in his division, he won. His name was Jake Burton Carpenter.

And the rest is snowboarding history.

While a handful of innovators from coast to coast were all busy pioneering snowboards throughout the 1970s, adding metal edges, bindings, boots, and other changes to the mix, the snowboard industry widely regards Sherm Poppen as the grandfather of the sport, and the Snurfer as the board that started it all.

Wendy's skis held together by two pieces of floor molding now reside in the Smithsonian Institution in Washington, D.C. Sherm is 81 years old, witty and self-effacing, and has been under doctor's orders not to snowboard since he was 78. He told us he got an e-mail from the Smithsonian telling him that his Snurfer would be on display in early 2012. "I told them I wanted to see my stuff on display before I die," he chuckled. "I guess they're honoring my wishes."

Forget for a second the half-billion-dollar industry that the Snurfer inspired. Forget Shaun White. Forget how, by some reports, the popularity of snowboarding since 2000 may have saved the ski resort industry. Instead, remember where it all began: with Sherm Poppen and two energetic daughters to delight. And note that 10,000 great work moments confirmed that Delivering the Difference makes our work 377 percent more likely to be considered important—or, in this case, cool and worth building on—by others.

DELIVER THE DIFFERENCE

Be obsessed with outcomes.
- Stay engaged. Stick it out. See it through.
- Don't stop until someone loves your work.

If your work isn't loved at first, fine-tune it for success.
- Have a growth mindset.
- See failures as progress toward learning what works.
- Chase what works. If something unexpected makes a difference, follow it.

Make one difference lead to another.
- Follow your work. Gather insights. Gain understanding.
- Insist on knowing what worked and why.
- See if one improvement holds clues to what's next.

Create great work that inspires others.
- Become sensitive to what people love.
- Improve your own difference-making ability.
- Become a catalyst for great work.

CONCLUSION

GET ON THE WALL

ONLY THE MOUNTAIN CAN TEACH US TO CLIMB IT.

It's true that choosing to become a difference maker involves some risk. After all, chasing ways in which we can improve the world is much more of an adventure than doing the same old same old. If we're looking for safety and security, the road to good work is well traveled and risk-free. If we're looking instead for growth, contribution, and success, the road to great work is paved with trial and error.

Even the difference-making skills, helpful as they are, can't be seen as a foolproof recipe for success. The best we can do is promise that great work is infinitely more engaging, exciting, and beneficial than good work, and that the difference-making skills will help our chances of doing great work rise exponentially. When it comes to scope, we don't need to reinvent the cell phone or create a billion-dollar app to do great work. The five skills can be applied to everything from the largest to the smallest of projects. The starting point is up to you. The important thing is to decide and begin.

· · ·

Todd Skinner was one of the most respected rock climbers of his generation. The subject of adventure films and magazine articles in media from ESPN to *Life*, he was famous for bold first ascents, daring expeditions, and redefining the word *impossible*. Based on his experience scaling the world's largest sheer granite walls, Todd gave us some advice we've never forgotten. He told us about his ascent of an improbable pillar of granite named Trango Tower.

Trango Tower is a 3,000-foot rocket-shaped spire in the Karakoram Range of the Himalayas. Its distinction as the world's highest freestanding spire, with a near-vertical drop, would make Trango Tower a difficult climb even if it were located in Yosemite, with campgrounds and grocery stores and showers nearby. In fact, Trango Tower is located in one of the most hostile, remote, and alien regions on the planet, making the climb even more ridiculously insane. When Todd went to find a sponsor for his expedition to free-climb the east face of Trango Tower, the sponsors consulted experts, and the experts declared the expedition impossible and thus un-fundable. A wall that big, in a place that remote, was simply not meant to be climbed.

But Todd's ultimately successful search for a sponsor was only a small part of preparing for his expedition. Finding the right climbing team took an exhaustive nationwide search. Planning logistics like travel, food, jeeps, porters, permits, weather, kerosene, equipment, first-aid supplies, clothing, and tents took years. Practicing climbing moves on boulders, short climbs, and other big walls to rehearse for Trango Tower took many more. But the real mental challenge wasn't overcoming the naysayers, doing finger pull-ups on doorjambs, or figuring out how many pounds of lentils and rice to bring along. The biggest mental challenge of the expedition came when, after years of preparation and a rugged 10-day cross-country trek through rivers and rocky terrain, the climbers came face-to-face with the largest, tallest, smoothest, steepest rock wall they had ever seen.

Todd describes the moment in his book, *Beyond the Summit,* "We turned a corner and there it was. The buttress dropped away, and Trango Tower rose stunningly before us. . . . The reality hit us like a shock wave. We stopped dead in the middle of the track, and the porters had to step around us. Each patted us on the back in passing, for no amount of bluff or bravado could hide the fact that we were absolutely horrified."

Trango Tower, Karakoram Range, Pakistan

The team members had intentionally come for the challenge, but now that they were face to face with the mountain, the challenge seemed too high, too vertical, too difficult, even for some of the best big wall climbers in the world. They sorted through their packs and laid out their equipment in the shadow of this amazing skyscraper of rock. And with what they hoped was a two-week climb of smooth golden granite looming above them, they hesitated. They kept looking up; counting their ropes; adjusting their harnesses; organizing their webbing, slings, cams, nuts, and bolts; and wondering if, after all, they should reconsider.

"We were apprehensive because there was so much we didn't know," Todd said. "When you set out to climb a mountain that has never been climbed, . . . you will realize at the base that you don't know how to get to the summit. But no amount of preparation before you arrive will give you all the answers."

In other words, Todd taught us that if we are truly attempting something new, there is no way to know beforehand if we have the skills to accomplish it. We can't know if it will work out. We don't even know if it's doable. Making the attempt is the only way to push the boundaries and discover what's truly possible. Sometimes we feel we are not good enough because the challenge is something harder than we've ever done before, Todd explained, "but that doesn't mean you can't become good enough. The improvement you need to reach the summit can only be gained on your way to the summit."

Todd told us how all people struggle, just like climbers, at the critical transition from the horizontal to the vertical—from preparation to action. "The final danger in the preparation process of an expedition is the tendency to postpone leaving until every question has been answered, forgetting that the mountain is the only place the answers can definitively be found. . . . No matter how well prepared you are, how honed your climbing skills, how vast your expertise, you cannot climb the mountain if you don't get to it."

In 1995, Todd and three teammates got to it and made the change from horizontal to vertical. In his terms, they "got on the wall." They had originally planned to spend 15 days above 18,500 feet on the face of Trango Tower, sleeping in tents suspended from the cliff wall as they slowly conquered the monolith one climbing pitch at a time. In the end, early snowstorms and the most difficult rock climbing in the world forced them to live on the wall, vertically, for 60 days before they finally reached the summit.

But they did it. And they made the April 1996 cover of *National Geographic*.

The mountain was their teacher. According to Todd, despite years of preparation and training, much of what they learned about climbing the tower was learned while they were on the wall.

The lesson for us is, we cannot become the difference makers we were meant to be until we leave the comfort of base camp and "get on the wall."

None of the great workers in this book knew everything they needed to know before they began—least of all whether the difference-making endeavor would be a success.

But every one of them got on the wall nonetheless.

They asked, saw, talked, improved, and delivered their way to great results. Whether it was the breakout success of the Polaroid Land Camera or Little Miss Matched or the personal fulfillment of Moses the janitor or Tina the photographer, the great work journey itself made them into the difference makers they had the potential to become. Then each of them, after making one difference, was determined to make another.

This leads to something we like to call "the life of a difference maker." It describes a phenomenon where someone makes a difference and is no longer content to rest on the laurels of that one-time accomplishment. We can become addicted to the rush of contributing more, producing new benefits, and delighting others with our work. Choosing to pursue the life of a difference maker encourages us to seek more and more difference-making opportunities, with bigger and better results. That's what the life of a difference maker looks like: a never-ending upward cycle of great work projects, each one cooler than the last.

A lifetime of learning, of contribution, of growth.

Who doesn't want that?

So whether your current difference-making impulse is a mild hankering or a fierce obsession, get on the wall. Reframe your role to become a difference maker. Work with what you've got. Ask the Right Question to discover what people would love. See for Yourself and Talk to Your Outer Circle to gather new ideas. Improve the Mix by adding, removing and checking for fit. And follow through to Deliver the Difference.

Finally, whether your great work journey is just beginning, or you have a recent innovation of your own to share, visit us at greatwork.com. We're constantly gathering and sharing examples of people doing great things to inspire difference makers like you. Because every time you make a difference, you make a contribution—to human progress, to the world around you, and to everyone who appreciates great work.

QUICK TAKE: HOW TO GET ON THE WALL

TAKE THE GREAT WORK CHALLENGE

If you'd like to involve a group of friends or coworkers in doing some great work, take the great work challenge.
- Invite your team to read *Great Work*.
- Get together and discuss its concepts, skills, and ideas.
- Apply the individual talents of team members to Ask the Right Question, See for Yourself, Talk to Your Outer Circle, Improve the Mix, and Deliver the Difference people love.
- Celebrate your success.

Pay special attention to that critical last step. When your team makes a difference, celebrate. And don't forget to share your success with us at greatwork.com.

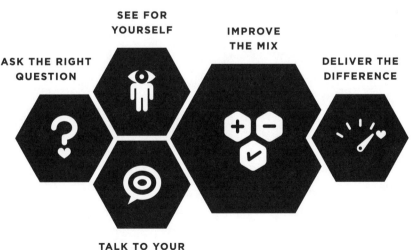

SEE FOR
YOURSELF

IMPROVE
THE MIX

ASK THE RIGHT
QUESTION

DELIVER THE
DIFFERENCE

TALK TO YOUR
OUTER CIRCLE

THE GREAT WORK STUDY

The Great Work study was the primary source of the five skills discussed in *Great Work*. This study, which began in early 2010, was designed by members and partners of the O.C. Tanner Institute to help us define "great work" and test the hypothesis that there are specific skills that anyone can practice to increase the odds of producing great work that others love.

In the Great Work study, we focused specifically on actions that led to great work, rather than using the traditional approach of looking at personality traits of high achievers. The Great Work study combined four disparate yet complementary research components: "The Executive Omnibus Survey" (Appendix A), "The O.C. Tanner Study of Award-Winning Work" (Appendix B), "The Forbes Insights Survey" (Appendix C), and "One-on-One Interviews" (Appendix D).

THE EXECUTIVE OMNIBUS SURVEY

We used the Executive Omnibus Survey to ask a diverse group of Harris Panel participants—302 senior executives from Fortune 100 companies—to give us their perspectives on great work and provide examples of great work in their organizations.

We asked executives: "When you think about great work in your organization, what comes to mind?" They responded with top-of-mind open-ended comments that fell naturally into two categories. The first was focused on "great work" the noun, or outcomes such as client satisfaction, product excellence, innovation, new product development, strategy execution, revenue growth, and profits. The second focused on "great work" as a verb, or how work is accomplished through teamwork, collaboration, communication, commitment, vision, passion, ownership, integrity, trust, planning, and ethics.

Another question we asked was, "Describe a project that represents great work to you." We have included a sample of the executives' responses here. Notice the prevalence of outcomes and differences made.

"We had a product developed many years ago that was underutilized. We modified it slightly and very quickly in response to a market need and have seen use and demand explode."

"Our company needed a way to track ROI. Someone built the systems and got buy-in to implement them. Now all projects have an ROI and a way for managers to track progress."

"Our service manager recognized an urgent customer need and organized multiple employees to pull together and surpass customer expectations."

"An employee figured out a way to speed up the processing of invoices. Invoices were manually paid, but the employee suggested an imaging sys tem, which produced faster processing of invoices."

"We came up with the idea for a new business line, took it to the top of the corporate ladder for approval, and then implemented the idea throughout the country at various levels. This new line helped our division to achieve the greatest growth rate in the history of the division."

"An employee developed a tool that beat all reporting capabilities of our standard ERP system. The interesting part is that no one asked him to do it or even looked into the possibility of developing something of that caliber."

"We have had some great contributions by new staff members creating models and procedures redefining how we approach our business and cli- ents. I've been very impressed by their energy and expertise."

"Someone developed a database that looked at customer spending behaviors and used that to identify opportunities to introduce them to new retailers. This generated new business for the retailers and a revenue stream for the company."

"We needed to improve sales lead generation. We created an improved process that increased the number of leads by 480 percent while maintaining lead quality above 60 percent."

"A colleague took on tasks beyond her responsibility to get a project moving in the right direction, then managed to transition responsibilities to the proper owner."

"A peer recently assisted our organization in entering a specific vertical that we had never sold to. She created a business plan and sold the opportunity to the board of directors. It has since turned into one of the largest verticals in our organization."

"Our supply chain organization identified the opportunity to save several million dollars in transportation costs by shifting the location of inventory."

THE O.C. TANNER STUDY
OF AWARD-WINNING WORK

The most far-reaching component of the Great Work study was our look into 1.7 million instances of award-winning work in corporations worldwide. In all, we pulled samples of 10,000 accounts of award-winning work.

These accounts came in the form of electronic nominations, written by supervisors or colleagues to describe what a person did to be deserving of a corporate award. Nominations averaged about 80 words in length. We analyzed an initial sample and coded its content into categories. These samples helped us focus on 19 variables of great work. To avoid subjectivity, two independent teams coded a final set of nominations from a uniform coding book with expanded definitions of the 19 most promising variables. The two coding efforts were then compared to ensure similarity of results. The average similarity of coding decisions was 80 percent between the two groups, a high level of intercoder reliability for such an exercise.

We created the nomination below as an example of a great work description as it might have been coded for the study.

NOMINATION FOR "JANE DOE":

	Sample Code:
Jane was made aware of a problem in our order entry system that was causing random customer orders to fail. In spite of all the other work on her plate, <u>she decided to fix the problem</u>.	-Initiative
Jane dove right in and <u>pulled together a cross-functional team</u> from several different departments.	-Connect with others
<u>She spent many hours analyzing log files</u> and assessing the root cause.	-Sacrifice made
In addition to fixing the core issues, she and her team <u>added a simple up-sell feature</u>.	-Combine new elements
Since the fix, order entries have returned to normal and <u>the up-sell feature generated $15,000 in new revenue last month</u>. I recommend that Jane receive a Gold Award for this accomplishment.	-Unexpected result

The following is a description of the research analysis method from Dr. Trent Kaufman and Lawrence Cowan of the Cicero Group, who ran a detailed analysis of the coded data.

The objective with the *Great Work* data set was to identify observed employee characteristics and traits that increase the chances (odds) an employee will produce great work.

The *Great Work* data set included dichotomous response variables, meaning the dependent variable (or response) was coded "1" when the characteristic was observed, and "0" when the characteristic was not observed. The use of dichotomous response variables is commonplace in the social sciences (for example, "employed" vs. "unemployed," "married" vs. "unmarried," "voted" vs. "didn't vote").

In the *Great Work* data set, response variables described aspects of an employee's observed outcome or the result of the work that was done, such as "made a financial impact," "had effect on others," etc.

Similarly, predictor variables described an employee's observed actions or causes of the result, such as "talked to their outer circle," "saw for themselves," etc.

The data was studied using a type of regression analysis known as a logit model (logit models were developed specifically for predicting outcomes of dichotomous response variables). The read-out from a logit model provides a measurement of the "odds" of an event occurring (similar to a probability).

The odds of an event is simply the ratio of the expected number of times an event will occur to the expected number of times it will not occur. For example, an odds of 3 means we can expect 3 times as many occurrences of the event as non-occurrences, where an odds of 1/4 means that we expect only one-fourth as many occurrences as non-occurrences.

With the *Great Work* data set, all coded "predictor = response" variables were tested as individual models. The data set included 5 response variables and 13 predictor variables, which produced 60 individual models. Of those models, 46 produced a statistically significant relationship between predictor and response variables with odds ratios ranging from 17.13 to 1.64. The most extreme case (17.13) can be explained as follows: An odds ratio of 17.13 informs us that the model predicts the odds of an employee having the "Passion" result (response variable) are 17.13 times higher for employees who have done the "See" action (predictor variable) than they are for employees who didn't do the "See" action.

Selected Findings:

Predictor Variable (ACTION)	Response Variable (RESULT)	Odds Ratio (LIKELIHOOD)
Ask the right question	Affects multiple people	4.12X
Ask the right question	Deemed important	3.13
Ask the right question	Creates passion	2.79
Ask the right question	Financial impact	2.69
Ask the right question	Unexpected positive	2.69

Predictor Variable (ACTION)	Response Variable (RESULT)	Odds Ratio (LIKELIHOOD)
See for yourself	Creates passion	17.13X
See for yourself	Positive emotion	11.80
See for yourself	Deemed important	3.60
See for yourself	Financial impact	3.57
See for yourself	Affects multiple people	2.42

Predictor Variable (ACTION)	Response Variable (RESULT)	Odds Ratio (LIKELIHOOD)
Talk to your outer circle	Financial impact	3.37X
Talk to your outer circle	Positive emotion	2.45
Talk to your outer circle	Affects multiple people	2.04

Predictor Variable (ACTION)	Response Variable (RESULT)	Odds Ratio (LIKELIHOOD)
Improve the mix	Deemed important	3.17X
Improve the mix	Financial impact	2.78
Improve the mix	Affects multiple people	2.10
Improve the mix	Positive emotion	1.75

Predictor Variable (ACTION)	Response Variable (RESULT)	Odds Ratio (LIKELIHOOD)
Deliver the difference	Deemed important	3.77X
Deliver the difference	Affects multiple people	3.18
Deliver the difference	Financial impact	1.99

ANOTHER WAY TO LOOK AT THE DATA

We analyzed the Great Work data set in many different ways. But one of the more interesting questions we asked was, "What happens to the odds of creating a result if two or more of the skills are present?" To answer this question, researchers looked at cases where more than one predictor variable (action) worked together and measured the combined effect on response variables (results). This is what we saw.

Selected Findings:

Predictor Variable (ACTION)	Response Variable (RESULT)	Odds Ratio (LIKELIHOOD)
Ask the right question Talk to your outer circle Deliver the difference	Financial impact	2.95X
Ask the right question Talk to your outer circle Improve the mix	Financial impact	4.32
Ask the right question Talk to your outer circle Improve the mix Deliver the difference	Financial impact	4.74

Predictor Variable (ACTION)	Response Variable (RESULT)	Odds Ratio (LIKELIHOOD)
Ask the right question Talk to your outer circle Improve the mix	Deemed important	6.54X
See for yourself Deliver the difference	Deemed important	6.68
See for yourself Talk to your outer circle Improve the mix Deliver the difference	Deemed important	10.53

Overall, the Great Work data set helped us understand what the five most important skills that affect great work are, and how the skills work together. In the previous charts, we can see that an employee is nearly five times more likely to affect bottom-line financial results if he or she is using the ask, talk, improve, and deliver skills together. Likewise, an employee is ten-and-a-half times more likely to do work that others consider important when he or she uses the see, talk, improve, and deliver skills in combination.

THE FORBES
INSIGHTS SURVEY

This survey focused on recent projects for hundreds of organizations in dozens of industries all over the world. Forbes asked 1,013 "employees," "supervisors," and "beneficiaries" to answer questions about specific projects delivered in the previous three months. The goal was to add clarity to our understanding of "great work" and to gather input about what causes it from a variety of relevant points of view.

We also sought to discover new insights that would validate (or invalidate) the five skills that were emerging from the O.C. Tanner Study of Award-Winning Work by varying the skill definitions and testing them alongside other potential predictors of great work.

Each survey asked participants to describe a recent project and rate its level of success from "far below expectations" to "far exceeds expectations." We categorized projects that "exceeded expectations" as great work, projects that "met expectations" as good work, and projects that "did not meet expectations" as poor work.

Through several pilot studies, we considered a wide range of survey questions that described each of the five skills. Statistical analysis allowed us to narrow down our list to a handful of survey questions that consistently and reliably described each of the five skills.

While the survey sought to clarify which skills were present when great work was achieved, it was also designed to help us see the degree to which those same skills were present during instances of good and poor work. Examples:

1. **ASK THE RIGHT QUESTION.** Two forms of asking what people would love showed up strongly in the questionnaires among employees: "I thought carefully about what would really make a difference" and "I gave a lot of thought to what outcome would delight the recipient of the work."

2. **SEE FOR YOURSELF.** The importance of looking to understand the work from the recipient's point of view came on strong here, as both beneficiaries and employees noted the value of "seeing from the vantage of those who receive the work."

3. **TALK TO YOUR OUTER CIRCLE.** The value of connecting "outside of one's regular team for insights," performed particularly strongly among beneficiaries of the work.

4. **IMPROVE THE MIX.** Two ideas that led us to the skill we called "Improve the Mix" were prevalent in the study. "I continued to shape my ideas and efforts until I felt they were right" and "I experimented with new techniques, strategies, and processes" both had a strong showing across all parties involved.

5. **DELIVER THE DIFFERENCE.** "I remained involved and engaged as the work product was delivered and implemented" scored only slightly higher than, "I felt a continued sense of ownership in the work as it was rolled out."

CASE STUDIES AND IN-DEPTH INTERVIEWS

In addition to the survey, Forbes Insights also conducted 360-degree interviews with "employees," "supervisors," and "beneficiaries" to showcase great work in action in four specific industries: automotive, publishing, high technology, and public relations. Business mogul Donald Trump, for example, offered Forbes Insights this definition: "Great work," he said, "implies going beyond what is expected and producing the unexpected."

ASK THE RIGHT QUESTION

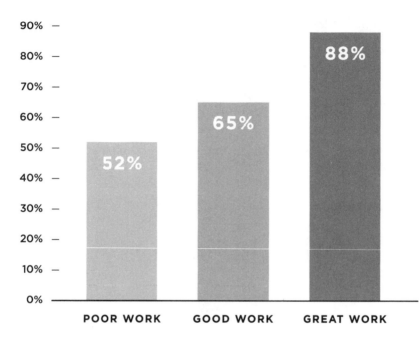

Nearly 9 out of every 10 instances of great work involved someone Asking the Right Question.

SEE FOR YOURSELF

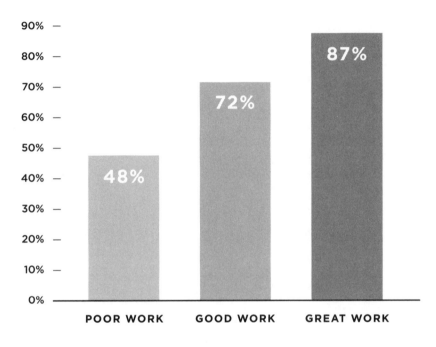

Nearly 9 out of every 10 instances of great work involved someone Seeing for Themselves what kind of changes or improvements might be loved by recipients of their work.

TALK TO YOUR OUTER CIRCLE

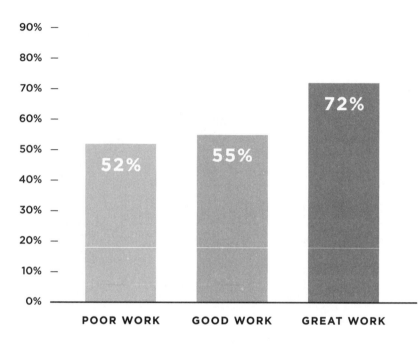

About 7 out of every 10 instances of great work involved people talking to others outside their usual team about the improvements that they were trying to make.

IMPROVE THE MIX

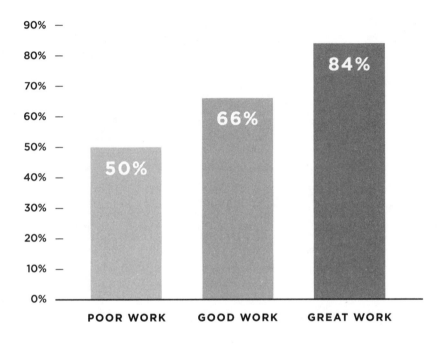

More than 8 out of every 10 instances of great work involved someone shaping and experimenting with ideas to make an improvement or add new value.

DELIVER THE DIFFERENCE

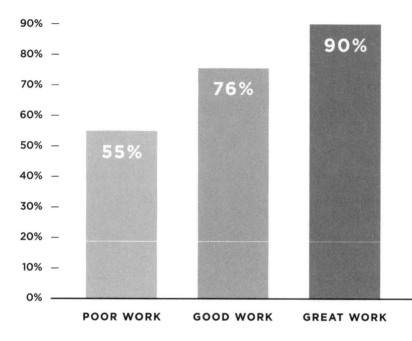

A full 9 out of every 10 instances of great work involved someone stay-ing involved, toughing it out, and seeing the work through to a desired result.

AN EXPLANATION OF "EXPLAINED VARIANCE"

One of the most exciting numbers from the Forbes Insights survey is 35 percent, which is the explained variance of the five skills working together. That means that people who start practicing these five skills together can expect their supervisors to notice a 35 percent increase in their production of work that exceeds expectations.

For those unfamiliar with "explained variance," Dr. Jeff Thompson of Brigham Young University provides this clarification:

When we say one thing affects another thing (like receiving a gift makes me happier), there is virtually never a 100% correlation. For instance, if we give someone a box of chocolates, we might brighten a rather gloomy day, but we probably won't get that person from despair to euphoria. The reason is that, aside from the chocolates, there are likely millions of other variables at work that affect the recipient's mood. It might be raining. They may have just stubbed their toe, or lost their dog, or eaten a bad lunch. In the face of all of that, if the gift of chocolates makes them 5% happier than they were before, they will probably be really grateful.

The data in the Forbes Insights survey is trying to predict how 5 skills impact outcomes that are based on human perception—like someone saying, "That work really exceeded my expectations." There is no possible way to capture 100% of the variables that might explain such a perception. A supervisor may want to view the work objectively, but a million other thoughts and influences like, "That wasn't anything like the idea I had," "he forgot my birthday last month," and "I hate people who wear purple" creep in. Social scientists call that "noise." To account for that "noise," explained variance is the statistical percentage of causation that we establish between X and Y. If explained variance is 15%, it means that X accounts for 15% of changes that happen to Y.

The Great Work study suggests that the five skills working together can fully explain more than a third of something as subjective as "great work." In other words, employees who engage in these five skills can expect supervisors to notice a 35 percent increase in their production of work that exceeds expectations. That's actually pretty incredible.

ONE-ON-ONE INTERVIEWS

The most qualitative component of our research consisted of more than 200 one-on-one interviews with people who were involved in great work that made a difference that was formally recognized. We investigated extraordinary outcomes large and small in dozens of different industries all over the world.

We interviewed a wide range of workers, from receptionists, call center agents, janitors, and pharmacists to innovators, including the inventor of the cell phone. By design, the volume of our interviews skewed toward everyday people who had made a difference others loved.

Interviews took place in person and by telephone and lasted anywhere from 30 minutes to four hours. Conversations focused on the great work accomplished, what happened, how it happened, and why. The interviews were open-ended, allowing each great work story to unfold naturally.

On the Nature of Great Work

"To do great work is to put your heart and soul into something. To not only do what you're told, but to put your stamp on something; to add a little extra; to have pride in your work."

"Work doesn't have to be drudgery. We don't have to wait around for something to happen. We can give ourselves the satisfaction of making something happen. This is fundamental to being human. We are all wired to do good."

"There's so much competition, we have to be different. And that's up to me. I make the difference."

"The idea of having created something, or having done something that is uniquely you, is what makes life worthwhile."

On Asking the Right Question

"Think about what would really impact those you serve and work for . . . and then 'backplan' to know what to do."

"I usually brainstorm each week. How can we do this? How can we get merchandise out and make it look great and not make a mess and not get in anyone's way? I pay close attention to how people react because sometimes you think something is amazing, but somebody else doesn't."

"I'm always considering options. Every time I talk to patients, I'm thinking, 'Would I do that for my mother?' If the answer is 'no,' then we are wasting that drug and we need to start over."

"The fun that you get out of doing something fun and unique and more than what people asked you to do ought to stimulate everybody."

"When I got the opportunity to manage the gift shop of a new hospital, I remembered all the months I spent in the hospital when my husband was dying of cancer. The gift shop was an escape for me. It was my getaway. Now I had the opportunity to create something that would affect somebody else in the same situation."

On Seeing for Yourself

"No consumer would have ever said in a focus group: I want 1,000 songs in my pocket. That idea was based upon seeing consumer behavior and taking the next logical step."

"We always ask employees what they want from our wellness program, but we also look at the data. If we see lots of heart disease or diabetes or issues with cholesterol in our company, we try to focus there."

"We took a trip to an auto dealer—because they do some pretty fancy finishes and trims and user interface stuff. We also looked at high-end stereo equipment. The controls on our washing machines were inspired by all those things."

"My team of HR generalists and I work on the floor at least twice a month with our employees. We get in uniform and get on the floor with them, cooking, cashiering, working graveyard shifts. It helps to see what our people are going through."

"As a clinical pharmacist, I don't just look at the one thing we are treating. I treat the whole patient. . . . I always look at their labs and every other test. "

"If there's a design-related issue that makes assembly difficult, you've got to watch somebody doing it, and work the problem on the spot. Sending a picture or a voice mail doesn't work. You've got to be there."

"I saw this vision of what could be and I didn't know how I was going to get there, but I just went for it and things began to happen."

On Talking to Your Outer Circle

"It's been about going out and talking with people and asking, 'What do you think would work? How do you see this happening?'"

"We're all creative, but there's not any one of us that has all the answers. So it's important to involve different points of view in order to get the creative solutions you need."

"There is a very natural, very human fear in sharing one's ideas. And yet it seems to be the x-factor, the differentiating thing."

"So this guy from Disney came in and he just said: 'Dude, you need some people who bring in unconventional thinking and that sort of stuff. And there are some great places you can get it.'"

"Desperation creates inspiration. . . . So I went and talked to our auto physical damage team to understand what they were doing. Communication is my bias. I always try to emphasize conversations."

"I managed across 10 silos, and that many people are inherently just not going to play nice together. So I had to basically build trust between them and me and amongst each other so that, together, we could invent some new ways to do things."

On Improving the Mix

"Most ideas aren't big grandiose ideas. They are little improvements."

"Any time you can take two things that people love—that they don't think *can* go together—and you somehow make them go together, you have a really great idea."

"We're a global company—but we don't always act that way. In this project, we were able to take designs of similar products in Brazil or China and kind of 'copy,' if you will, their designs to leverage our global expertise."

"I'm always a believer that there's a better way to do things."

"There is more than one way of doing things. Great work is about finding the unique path, the different approach, that will make a difference."

"I fill my mind with possibilities, and then just hook them together."

On Delivering the Difference

"We knew if we could just work through a few more problems, we were going to get there. Our team got labeled 'the dragon slayers' for the way we worked those issues."

"We were getting the paperwork together when we realized we were going to be zero landfill after today. But we decided to wait to make sure it was real. Each week would tick by and we were still zero landfill. So finally we felt comfortable announcing that we did it."

"There were so many people who thought what I was doing was a neat idea—in every corner of the world. But nobody had gone from the hobby stage to the commercial stage."

"We gain satisfaction from helping others and accomplishing something—we're wired that way. But we have to build or create something. We need to make things happen."

"You cannot learn anything unless you make a mistake. So what I tell my students is, if you make a mistake, the thing to do is to celebrate and think, 'how fascinating.'"

"The guy who was in charge of quality was just rabid on understanding what customers were saying and getting that info immediately back to the person who could do something about it."

NOTES AND RESOURCES

Great Work is the result of more than three years of research and interviews with academic advisors, business executives, award-winning employees, and difference makers conducted by members of the O.C. Tanner Institute. In addition, we learned from the writings of many authors, researchers, biographers, historians, reporters, and thought leaders who confirmed or enriched our findings on great work—some of whom were quoted in the text.

The following is a list of primary sources, accreditations, and acknowledgments, including a few sources that were not used in *Great Work* that may be of interest for further reading or study. Because many of these articles and studies are available online, we have attempted to provide enough information to make them easily accessible via an Internet search.

INTRODUCTION: THE INCREDIBLE DISAPPEARING SCHOOL

Skip Hults's story was created from a series of interviews. You can learn more about the impact of Skip's international student program by listening to or reading a transcript of Brian Mann's NPR story "Rural New York School Recruits Overseas Students." Town Supervisor George Cannon's quote comes from the end of the broadcast. For further study, Stephanie Simon's story for Reuters, "Insight: Public Schools Sell Empty Classroom Seats Abroad," talks about the impact of international public school programs beyond Newcomb, New York. Public Radio International also has an excellent story titled "Rural Schools Recruit International Students to Raise Money."

WHERE THIS BOOK COMES FROM

Please refer to the appendices for an insightful overview of the Great Work research project.

HOW DIFFERENCE MAKERS THINK

Ed's story was told entirely from a series of interviews.

We also interviewed Dr. Jane Dutton and Justin Berg on multiple occasions. A detailed article on the team's job crafting work was published in *Academy of Management Review* 26, no. 2, 2001, pp. 179–201. Amy, Jane, and Justin also wrote an article titled "Turn the Job You Have into the Job You Want," published in the *Harvard Business Review,* June 2010, pp. 114–117. Jane and Justin told us about "reframing," which is described alongside other forms of job crafting in an article by Justin, Jane, and Amy titled "Perceiving and Responding to Challenges in Job Crafting at Different Ranks" in the *Journal of Organizational Behavior* 31, no. 2–3, 2010, pp. 158–186.

Mindi shared the story of Moses with us in several personal interviews.

The story of Dr. Seuss was researched from multiple sources including "Why Johnny Can't Read," *Time* magazine, 1955; Lynn Neary's great

NPR story, *Fifty Years of Cat in the Hat*; Stacy Conradt's *Ten Stories Behind Dr. Seuss Stories* on WSJ.com (reprinted there by permission from mentalfloss.com). Also see L. Gordon Crovitz's *Wall Street Journal* article, "E-Seuss: Be Glad. Not Sad or Mad"; Erin Anderson's story in the *Lincoln (Nebraska) Star Journal*, "Who Let the Cat In?"; and Pamela Paul's *New York Times* story, "The Children's Authors Who Broke All the Rules." Two well-researched books proved useful for fact-checking and are recommended reading for Seuss fans: Phillip Nel's *The Annotated Cat* (New York: Random House, 2007) and Donald E. Pease's *Theodor SEUSS Geisel* (New York: Oxford University Press, 2010).

The Frank Gehry quote comes from an interview in Academy of Achievement, 1995; www.achievement.org/autodoc/page/geh0int-1.

The Lego fact comes from Tracy V. Wilson's "How Lego Bricks Work" at howstuffworks.com. The mathematicians responsible for the number explain their equation here: http://www.math.ku.dk/~eilers/lego.html #howgetright.

ASK THE RIGHT QUESTION

Rob Burns was kind enough to share the great work that he and his team did at The Hartford in three separate interviews and many follow-up phone calls.

Having cofounded LittleMissMatched Inc. in 2004, Jonah Staw is the company's CEO. We learned about Jonah's entrepreneurial undertaking from the online articles "Mismatched Sock Company Puts Entrepreneurial Foot Forward: LittleMissMatched," nyreport.com;

and Abby Ellin, "A (Mis)Match for Tough Times," cbsnews.com. You can learn more about the company at littlemissmatched.com and at its YouTube channel.

The impact of Edwin Land and the company, Polaroid, continues to ripple into new technologies. For information on Edwin's invention of the Polaroid Land Camera, we referenced Joyce Furstenau, "The Polaroid Camera," edhelper.com; F. W. Campbell, FRS, "Instant Photography," rowland.harvard.edu; "Edwin Herbert Land," robinson-library.com; and "Edwin H. Land Is Dead at 81: Inventor of Polaroid Camera," nytimes.com.

The unlikely impact of Friday night dinner dances on retention at a manufacturing plant in Guadalajara, Mexico, was shared in an interview with Mike Collins, the great worker who came up with the idea.

We interviewed Annette Gertge several times. Each time, she emphasized the fact that the safe disassembling of her company's plating room, and the millions saved, was not because of her great work. It was all due to the exceptional people on her team.

We were fortunate enough to interview Martin Cooper twice as we gathered information on the invention of the cell phone and its impact on the world. We also referenced two online videos: Bob Greene, "38 Years Ago He Made the First Cell Phone Call," cnn.com; and "The Cell Phone: Marty Cooper's Big Idea," *60 Minutes*, cbsnews.com.

The quote from *Babe* comes from the 1995 motion picture produced by Kennedy Miller Productions and distributed by Universal Pictures.

SEE FOR YOURSELF

The true source of Wayne Gretzky's most famous quote is explained in detail in Jill Rosenfeld's amusing article, "CDU to Gretzky: The Puck Stops Here!," *Fast Company*, June 2000. Incidentally, Walter Gretzky's actual quote does not end with "where it is," as commonly quoted, but with "where it has been." The story of Wayne's tracing the puck is told in many places, including Dave Naylor, "Gretzky's Name Still Resonates with Us," TSN.com, among others. We quoted the version told by Walter Gretzky to Joe O'Conner for the *National Post* on April 18, 2012.

The mental picture of Jack Nicklaus walking Red Ledges golf course was inspired by Mike Stansfield's article for *Fairways* magazine entitled "Red Ledges: The Anatomy of a Golf Course." Facts about Jack's career were found at his corporate website, www.nicklaus.com.

The IDEO/Evenflo stroller partnership was written from our experience on-site at IDEO with facts verified at IDEO.com.

Jim Cook's visit to post offices for Netflix was told by Jim Cook in an article titled, "Five Lessons from the Netflix Startup Story" on marketingprofs.com. Both quotes are from this article.

Eiji Naktsu's discovery of the Kingfisher nose for the bullet train was inspired by EarthSky's interview with Sunni Robertson of the San Diego Zoo, "Sunni Robertson on How a Kingfisher Inspired a Bullet Train." We were fortunate to interview Eiji online via an interpreter for the details of his story. To see other examples of biomimicry, view the slideshow at http://www.treehugger.com/slideshows/clean-technology/nature -inspired-innovation-9-examples-of-biomimicry-in-action/#slide-top.

We interviewed Denise Coogan many times about her team's success in making Subaru of Indiana a zero landfill facility, including an inspirational trip to the factory to see the team's work for ourselves.

The Edna Mode quotes are, of course, from the 2004 Disney/Pixar movie *The Incredibles*.

Pierre Crevier told us in an interview about how the Whirlpool "Git It Done" project was transformed into a brilliant renaissance for the top-load washer.

The Dutch bicycle culture was experienced firsthand by a member of the O.C. Tanner institute and fact-checked via a number of sources, including Russell Shorto's *New York Times* story, "The Dutch Way: Bicycles and Fresh Bread" (July 30, 2011); John Pucher and Ralph Buehler, "Making Cycling Irresistible: Lessons from the Netherlands, Denmark, and Germany," *Transport Reviews* 28, no. 4, 2008, pp. 495–528); a presentation by Cor Van Der Klaauw posted at http://www.fietsberaad .nl/library/repository/bestanden/document000113.pdf; and a tremendous article by Mark Jenkins, "The Way It Should Be Is the Way It Is," for *Bicycling*, June 2008.

TALK TO YOUR OUTER CIRCLE

We learned of the connection between mosquitoes, plastic bags, and malaria from O.C. Tanner Institute contributor Julia Lapine. You can read more about Wengari Maathai and the Green Belt Movement she founded in Africa here: http://www.seeafricadifferently.com/news /wangari-maathai-african-hero. If you're interested in the subject of neuroplasticity, we suggest the following resources: *Brain Rules*, by John Medina (Pear Press, 2009); *The Brain That Changes Itself*, by Norman Doidge, MD (Penguin, 2007); *Magnificent Mind at Any Age*, by Daniel G. Amen, MD (Three Rivers Press, 2009); *How God Changes Your Brain*, by Andrew Newberg, MD and Mark Robert Waldman (Ballantine, 2010); *The Human Brain Book*, by Rita Carter (DK Adult, 2009); *The Brain*, The History Channel (video), *The Secret Life of the Brain*, PBS (video). The "neurobiology of we" quote by Dr. Daniel Siegel comes from a two-day seminar in 2010 titled The Mind That Changes The Brain, as quoted in an article by Patty de Llosa for *Parabola* at http://www.parabola.org/the-neurobiology-of-we.html. The number of words we speak each day was written about by Nikhil Swaminathan in "Gender Jabber: Do Women Talk More than Men?," *Scientific American,* July 6, 2007, http://www.scientificamerican.com/article.cfm?id=women-talk-more-than-men.

You can read more about the size of our inner circle in Paul Adams' *Grouped: How Small Groups Of Friends Are The Key To Influence On The Social Web*, Chapter 2 (New Riders, 2012). John Kreiser's article for CBS News, "Is Your Circle Of Friends Shrinking?," February 11, 2009, suggests our circle of confidants is even smaller, having dropped by one entire person (from 3 to 2) from 1985 to 2004.

We reconstructed the story of Rob Burns connecting with his inner and outer circles at The Hartford from several one-on-one interviews with Rob.

We first met Ben Zander when he came to speak at O.C. Tanner's eightieth anniversary. Having read his book *The Art of Possibility: Transforming Professional and Personal Life*, by Rosamund Stone

Zander and Benjamin Zander (Boston: Harvard Business School Press, 2000), we recalled his story about white sheets. In a personal interview with him, we learned more about the difference his idea has made. You can view Ben online at: "Benjamin Zander: The Transformative Power of Classical Music," ted.com; "Benjamin Zander: A True Leader," youtube.com; and "The Art of Possibility," youtube.com.

We learned about Ed Melcarek and Colgate from Jeff Howe's "The Rise of Crowdsourcing" for *Wired* magazine, June 2006. Additional details came from www.ideaconnection.com. If crowdsourcing interests you, we suggest you read *Crowdsourcing,* by Jeff Howe (Crown Business, 2009). The Karim Lakhani quote comes from his paper *The Value of Openness in Scientific Problem Solving* (Lakhani, Jeppesen, Lohse, Panetta, 2007). More on Mark Granovetter's studies on social network theory may be discovered by reading "The Strength of Weak Ties: A Network Theory Revisited," Mark Granovetter, http://sociology .stanford.edu/people/mgranovetter/documents/granstrengthweakties .pdf. We also recommend, *Getting a Job: A Study of Contacts and Careers*, by Mark Granovetter (University of Chicago Press, 1995).

Several of us at O.C. Tanner are lenders on Kiva.org. Inspired by the difference that Kiva is making, we found it to be an exceptional example of great work. The following online articles and videos were referenced in telling Matt Flannery and Jessica Jackley's story: Matt Flannery, "Kiva and the Birth of Person-to-Person Microfinance," *Innovations*, Winter/Spring 2007; Matt Flannery, "Kiva at Four," *Innovations*, Skoll World Forum 2009; "Jessica Jackley: Poverty, Money, and Love," ted .com; "The Story of Kiva," youtube.com; and "Intercontinental Ballistic Microfinance: A Wonderful Visualization," *The Atlantic*, September 1, 2011.

IMPROVE THE MIX

Dan Gilbert's quote on the workings of the prefrontal cortex comes from his great TED talk, "The Surprising Science of Happiness," ted.com.

The origins of storyboarding at Disney studios are catalogued in Diane Disney Miller, *The Story of Walt Disney* (New York: Henry Holt, 1956); John Canemaker, *Paper Dreams: The Art and Artists of Disney Storyboards* (New York: Hyperion Press, 1999); and Christopher Finch, *The Art of Walt Disney* (New York: Abrams, 1974).

David's scout committee came from an O.C. Tanner Institute member's firsthand account.

James Dyson's removal of the vacuum cleaner bag is widely chronicled. We learned the history of his invention at dyson.com and quoted James from a video under the link "A New Idea." You can also learn more at http://www.fastcompany.com/fast50_04/winners/dyson.html, and from James Dyson, *Against the Odds: An Autobiography* (New York: Texere, 2000).

We were first introduced to Miguel's inspiring work at Veta La Palma fish farm by viewing Dan Barber's entertaining TED talk, "How I Fell in Love with a Fish," quoted twice in the text. We were lucky to interview Miguel on many occasions, including a personal visit to Veta La Palma in late 2012. The farm is incredible. You can also learn more by reading Lisa Abend, "Sustainable Aquaculture: Net Profits," *Time*, June 15, 2009.

We were fortunate to hear the Nike+ story from Curt Roberts, who was kind enough to grant an interview.

The rest of Skip Hults's success story with the international students at Newcomb School was put together from the aforementioned interviews.

Having first heard about the Green Microgym in a *Wired* magazine article entitled, "For Fitness Fanatics, Old-Style Gyms Don't Cut It Anymore," we reached out to Adam Boesel and interviewed him for *Great Work.*

DELIVER THE DIFFERENCE

For the anecdote about Bill Klem, we referenced several articles: Nick Paumgarten, "No Flag on the Play," newyorker.com; "Bill Klem," baseball-reference.com; "Bill Klem," baseballhall.org; and "Bill Klem," en.wikipedia.org.

Tina Rossi, a portrait photographer for Lifetouch, shared her great work story with us in an interview.

Carol Dweck's growth mindset studies have been widely written about. We first discovered them via Po Bronson's story "How Not to Talk to Your Kids," *New York*, August 3, 2007, then we saw them in "Dr. Carol Dweck on Fixed vs. Growth Mindsets," youtube.com, and Maria Krakovsky, "The Effort Effect," *Stanford Magazine,* March/April 2007. But you can learn more about Carol's work from the website mindset online.com, which is filled with useful links, and Carol's book, *Mindset: The New Psychology of Success* (New York: Ballantine, 2007).

Given that great work is so often a journey that takes iteration and refinements, we were struck by the journey from Burbn to Instagram. In telling Kevin Systrom's story, we referenced the following articles and videos: Dominic Rushe, "Instagram Founders Turn Two Years of Work into $1bn—Only in Silicon Valley," guardian.co.uk; Kim-Mai Cutler, "From 0 to $1 Billion in Two Years: Instagram's Rose-Tinted Ride to Glory," techcrunch.com; M. G. Siegler, "Distilled from Burbn, Instagram Makes Quick Beautiful Photos Social," techcrunch.com; Somini Sengupta, "Behind Instagram's Success, Networking the Old Way," nytimes.com; "The Startup That Died So Instagram Could Live," money .cnn.com; "Kevin Systrom Says Comparing Instagram to Photography Is Like 'Comparing Twitter to Microsoft Word,'" techland.time.com; "The Story of Instagram," iitstories.com; "Kevin Systrom on Instagram's Meteoric Rise . . . and When Is It Coming to Android?," thenextweb.com; and Kevin Rose, "Foundation 16//Kevin Systrom," youtube.com.

While Mike explained the process of improving the electrobonding welding machine here at O.C. Tanner, he was quick to point out that it was a team of researchers, welders, process owners, and statisticians that increased the success rate of welds to 99 percent.

The grandfather of snowboarding, Sherm Poppen, shared his difference-making story with us in multiple delightful interviews.

GET ON THE WALL

Mountain climber Todd Skinner came to speak at O.C. Tanner in 1999. It was a pivotal moment in the company's history. We were embarking on a massive enterprise resource planning project and needed encouragement. His phrase, "get on the wall," has become a rallying cry of sorts that is part of our culture to this day. Todd passed away in 2006 when his equipment failed during a routine rappel in Yosemite National Park. While the story in this book is very much like the one he shared in person, we recreated it with quotes from Todd's excellent management book, *Beyond the Summit* (New York: Portfolio Hardcover, 2003) and his story of climbing Trango Tower in *National Geographic* (April 1996). To the climbing community, and the corporations he inspired, Todd was a difference maker of the highest order.

ACKNOWLEDGMENTS

Great Work was a team effort. I want to make that perfectly clear. To that end, there are many people I would like to thank.

In the first place, I would like to thank the people we interviewed for this book. They are its true heroes. Some of their names made it into the book; others, too numerous to mention, did not. But it was these actual doers of great work who opened our eyes, schooled us, and helped us identify patterns of difference-making behaviors.

Next, I'd like to thank the talented team of both members and partners of the O.C. Tanner Institute that created this book with me (hence, the name of the institute on the cover).

Four coauthors worked so closely with me on the content of *Great Work* that I feel I owe them special appreciation.

Dr. Barclay Burns was my first collaborator. While working on a second PhD (this one in strategy at Cambridge), Barclay brought enthusiasm and academic research to bear on the earliest conversations about great work. In those early whiteboard sessions, we modeled frameworks of value creation; mapped the way people think, learn, and develop; and discussed the psychology of human accomplishment. These ideas formed some of the early hypotheses for *Great Work*. Barclay attended workshops, reviewed manuscripts, and offered insights. Nearly three years later, I can look at *Great Work* and see ideas inspired by those early meetings.

Mark Cook, a published author in his own right, joined the project by reading a mountain of academic studies and business books to bring us up to speed on third-party research. Then Mark dove in to the great work database, organizing the team that spent hundreds of hours reading and coding thousands of instances of great work. He hired researchers to run regression models. He did analyses. He formulated new studies. And all the while, he was making time to conduct 200 one-on-one interviews. It was Mark's heavy lifting on primary and secondary research that uncovered and defined the five difference-making skills. Mark also developed workshops and training exercises with more than 400 participants. These experiences with real audiences helped us test, refine, and communicate the ideas that became *Great Work*.

Chris Drysdale and Todd Scurr, two accomplished creative directors, took on the bulk of the writing. Both friends added valuable insights from their creative professions. I value their strategic direction, critical thinking, and idea-generating capabilities. Todd's understanding of what makes people tick brought a human, personal touch to *Great Work*. Chris's keen ear helped us strip away unnecessary facts and get to the heart of exactly what needed to be said. I owe an apology to both of them for missed vacations, lost weekends, and sacrificed sleep. These two killed themselves to research, interview, and write stories, often to throw them out and replace them without complaint. Chris and Todd filled the blank pages, kept the dream alive during tough times, and stuck it out until a difference was made. Whenever people tell me that this book is "a great read," I give a thankful nod to Todd and Chris. In the end, I owe Chris special thanks for taking on the task of bringing it all together. While deftly making the work of multiple contributors come together as one, he also found a way to give the book the right creative voice.

Our research team spent countless hours reading thousands of cases of award-winning work to code and analyze the data. Thanks to Gary Beckstrand, Christina Chau, David Rosenlund, Chris Berry, Sean Branigan, Mercedes White, Matt Fereday, and Matt Dever. Also thanks to the professionals at Cicero Research, especially Dr. Trent Kaufman and Lawrence Cowan, plus the research team at Forbes Insights, including Hannah Seligson, Brenna Sniderman, Kasia Moreno, and Christiaan Rizy. Doctors Jeff Thompson and Stuart Bunderson, both experts in organizational behavior, worked with us from the beginning to help us formulate questions and develop testing methods.

Our graphic designers, Julia LaPine and Scott Arrowood, joined the team early to help with critical thinking, creative insights, and idea generation. They were then called upon to add graphic design elements: type, infographics, and cover art. Alisha Newbold was our tireless project manager, organizing workshops, managing logistics, ideating exercises, producing materials, and keeping the rest of us crazies organized. A talented group of contributing editors helped us find and compose stories and experiment with early chapter outlines. Thanks to Pamela Mason Davey, Christy Anderson, Mindi Cox, Todd Nordstrom, and Charlotte Evans. I'd like to thank Emily Loose, whose critical edit of an early draft made the manuscript so much cleaner and smarter. And special thanks to Donya Dickerson, executive editor at McGraw-Hill, who worked through all the final meticulous edits that brought the book home.

Along the way, I bounced ideas off many trusted colleagues and friends. These people listened thoughtfully and always found a way to contribute valuable ideas. Thanks to Mike Collins, John McVeigh, Tim

Treu, Brian Katz, Beth Thornton, Charlotte Miller, Dave Hilton, Gary Peterson, Scott Jensen, Scott Sperry, Joel Dehlin, Michelle Smith, Rob Mukai, Sandra Christensen, Allison VanVranken, Rex Remigi, Kevin Curtis, Ed Bagley, Heather McArthur, Jarond Suman, Kevin Ames, Shauna Bona, Angie Hagen, and Mary Robins, who always keeps me out of trouble. Thanks also to the O.C. Tanner security team, who stayed until 2:00 a.m. every time we did.

Thanks to Kent Murdock, former CEO of O.C. Tanner, for his early belief in *Great Work*. And to Dave Petersen, current CEO of O.C. Tanner, who sponsored and encouraged *Great Work* as only a great leader can. Thanks for allowing me to divide my attention between *Great Work* and my day job. Your frequent ribbing for my disappearances related to this project was well deserved. The first copy goes to you.

I would also like to thank my dad, George, whose analytical mind taught me to be fascinated by how things work, and my mom, Louise, a difference maker through and through who passed away during the writing of this book. Her life was a monument to doing things other people loved.

Finally, to my wife, Stacie, for being my biggest believer, most patient listener, and wisest advisor—all the while being there at parent-teacher conferences, soccer games, tennis matches, recitals, and birthday parties when I could not. And thanks to our children, Benton, Sarah, Emma, and Olivia, who wonder if I will ever stop sharing great work stories at the dinner table. Sorry, kids. Probably not.

INDEX

University of Michigan, 7
unknown land, 27

V

vacuum, 114–116
variables in Great Work study,
    175–179
variance, explained, 189–190
Veta La Palma fishery, 117–123

W

Wallage, Jacques, 72
Walt Disney Studios, 104–105
washing machines, 68–70
waste
    plastic bags and malaria, 76–77
    Subaru's zero landfill initiative,
        61–67

welding, 149–152
Whirlpool, 68–70
white sheets, 90–91
Wild Bird Society of Japan, 60
Wired, 90
Workers Compensation Fund,
    41
Wrzesniewski, Amy, 7

Y

Yamana, Masao, 61
yearbook photography, 141–144
Yunus, Dr. Muhammad, 96

Z

Zander, Benjamin, 89–91
zero landfill initiative, 61–67

ABOUT THE AUTHOR

David Sturt is an Executive Vice President of the O.C. Tanner Company. His career began in market research, where he analyzed the impact of recognition on people and their work. In the two decades since, he has developed products and services that engage employees, inspire contribution, and reward outstanding results in organizations around the world. He regularly consults with Fortune 1000 leaders and speaks to audiences worldwide. He has been interviewed by the *Wall Street Journal*, MSNBC, *Human Capital*, and is a guest contributor for Forbes.com.

O.C. TANNER INSTITUTE

The mission of the O.C. Tanner Institute is to research and share insights that help organizations inspire and appreciate great work. The institute provides a global forum for exchanging ideas about recognition, engagement, leadership, culture, human values, and sound business principles.

For information on speaking engagements and workshops, visit greatwork.com.